Germs

Other books in the Great Medical Discoveries series:

Great Medical Discoveries

Germs

by Don Nardo

On cover: An *E coli* bacterium magnified 5,000 times.

LIBRARY OF CONGRESS CATALOGING-IN-PUBLICATION DATA

Nardo, Don, 1947—
    Germs / by Don Nardo.
        v. cm. — (Great medical discoveries)
    Includes bibliographical references and index.
    Contents: An invisible world revealed—Early attempts to explain disease—The modern discovery of germs—The germ theory proven at last—Disease detectives track down germs—A host of beneficial germs—Germs as weapons: Biological warfare.
        ISBN 1-59018-255-3 (hardback : alk. paper)
    1. Germ theory of disease—Juvenile literature. 2. Microbiology—Juvenile literature [1. Germ theory of disease. 2. Microbiology.] I. Title. II. Series
        RB153.N37 2003
        616'.01—dc21
                                                                    20021544435

Printed in the United States of America

CONTENTS

FOREWORD

Throughout history, people have struggled to understand and conquer the diseases and physical ailments that plague us. Once in a while, a discovery has changed the course of medicine and sometimes, the course of history itself. The stories of these discoveries have many elements in common—accidental findings, sudden insights, human dedication, and most of all, powerful results. Many illnesses that in the past were essentially a death warrant for their sufferers are today curable or even virtually extinct. And exciting new directions in medicine promise a future in which the building blocks of human life itself—the genes—may be manipulated and altered to restore health or to prevent disease from occurring in the first place.

It has been said that an insight is simply a rearrangement of already-known facts, and as often as not, these great medical discoveries have resulted partly from a reexamination of earlier efforts in light of new knowledge. Nineteenth-century monk Gregor Mendel experimented with pea plants for years, quietly unlocking the mysteries of genetics. However, the importance of his findings went unnoticed until three separate scientists, studying cell division with a newly improved invention called a microscope, rediscovered his work decades after his death. French doctor Jean-Antoine Villemin's experiments with rabbits proved that tuberculosis was contagious, but his conclusions were politely ignored by the medical community until another doctor, Robert Koch of Germany, discovered the exact culprit—the tubercle bacillus germ—years later.

Accident, too, has played a part in some medical discoveries. Because the tuberculosis germ does not stain with dye as easily as other bacteria, Koch was able to see it only after he had let a treated slide sit far longer than he intended. An unwanted speck of mold led Englishman Alexander Fleming to recognize the bacteria-killing qualities of the penicillium fungi, ushering in the era of antibiotic "miracle drugs."

That researchers sometimes benefited from fortuitous accidents does not mean that they were bumbling amateurs who relied solely on luck. They were dedicated scientists whose work created the conditions under which such lucky events could occur; many sacrificed years of their lives to observation and experimentation. Sometimes the price they paid was higher. Rene Launnec, who invented the stethoscope to help him study the effects of tuberculosis, himself succumbed to the disease.

And humanity has benefited from these scientists' efforts. The formerly terrifying disease of smallpox has been eliminated from the face of the earth—the only case of the complete conquest of a once deadly disease. Tuberculosis, perhaps the oldest disease known to humans and certainly one of its most prolific killers, has been essentially wiped out in some parts of the world. Genetically engineered insulin is a godsend to countless diabetics who are allergic to the animal insulin that has traditionally been used to help them.

Despite such triumphs there are few unequivocal success stories in the history of great medical discoveries. New strains of tuberculosis are proving to be resistant to the antibiotics originally developed to treat them, raising the specter of a resurgence of the disease that has killed 2 billion people over the course of human history. But medical research continues on numerous fronts and will no doubt lead to still undreamed-of advancements in the future.

Each volume in the Great Medical Discoveries series tells the story of one great medical breakthrough—the first gropings for understanding, the pieces that came together and how, and the immediate and longer-term results. Part science and part social history, the series explains some of the key findings that have shaped modern medicine and relieved untold human suffering. Numerous primary and secondary source quotations enhance the text and bring to life all the drama of scientific discovery. Sidebars highlight personalities and convey personal stories. The series also discusses the future of each medical discovery—a future in which vaccines may guard against AIDS, gene therapy may eliminate cancer, and other as-yet unimagined treatments may become commonplace.

INTRODUCTION

An Invisible World Revealed

Germs are the oldest living things on Earth, literally billions of years older than mammals, including the most highly advanced mammal—humans. Therefore, early humans, other mammals, and their more primitive ancestors all lived out their lives with germs on them, inside them, and inhabiting every conceivable niche of the environment around them. Some of these germs were harmless and simply coexisted with plants and animals. Others proved more dangerous by infecting and killing other living things. Indeed, diseases caused by germs are nothing new, as noted science writer Arno Karlen points out in his popular book *Man and Microbes*:

> Infection was already ubiquitous [existing everywhere] when higher organisms left their first fossil traces, some half a billion years ago. There are fossil plants with fossil fungus infections, and ancient jellyfish and mollusks bearing signs of parasites. Dinosaur bones 250 million years old have marks of bacterial infection, as do the remains of mastodons [early elephants] and saber-tooth tigers. . . . Our [human] ancestors probably suffered as many diseases, new and old, as did other mammals. . . . Whether these were the same microbes that exist today is not certain, but fossils speak eloquently of ancient trauma and infection. . . . We cannot be sure that exactly the same germs afflicted dinosaurs and Neanderthalers [an

extinct race of humans], but even if the germs were not identical, the process must have been similar.[1]

As happens today, animals and people were able to develop resistances to certain diseases over time. So a germ that wiped out hundreds of early humans when they first encountered it might, after the passage of a few thousand years, become less dangerous and fade into the ever-present mixture of harmless germs swirling around humans. However, exposure to new germs was inescapable. This was especially true when primitive humans underwent major changes in their living habits. Again, some of the new germs they encountered were harmless, even beneficial; but others were not. "The first big shock to influence human disease patterns," Karlen suggests, "was our ancestors' descent from the trees to the ground, about five million years ago," which "freed them from some old diseases but exposed them to new ones, through ground-level air, water, and foods. . . . Being new to people, the germs often caused far worse symptoms than in their usual hosts."[2]

The agricultural revolution, which occurred perhaps ten to twelve thousand years ago in the Middle East, likely brought our ancestors into contact with so many new germs that, Karlen quips, it is amazing that humanity managed to survive at all. Much of this onslaught of new diseases was the result of close contact with newly domesticated animals. According to Karlen, diseases such as influenza measles, mumps, and smallpox probably first came from these animals:

> The measles germ is related to the viruses causing distemper in dogs, rinderpest in cattle, and a type of swine fever; any of these may have sparked the human disease, though the distemper virus seems the best candidate. The smallpox virus is kin to those causing vaccinia in cows, ectromedia in mice, and pox infections in fowl and swine. Such zoonoses [animal diseases] ticked away in

village and barnyard, biological bombs awaiting dense human populations.[3]

No Knowledge of Germs or Hygiene

It did not take long for those dense human populations to materialize, because the first cities appeared only a few thousand years after the advent of agriculture. One by one the waiting "biological bombs" exploded, creating the first major epidemics to afflict the human race. The people who survived such plagues did not realize that germs had attacked them, of course. After all, germs are far too tiny to see with the unaided eye; throughout most of human history people had no clue that their bodies, clothes, homes, animals, crops, and practically everything else were crawling with microscopic creatures, most of them harmless but a few of them deadly.

An ancient Egyptian couple use oxen to plow their field. Many of the diseases that afflicted early humans came from contact with domesticated animals.

Because they knew nothing about the existence of germs, ancient peoples searched for other explanations for outbreaks of debilitating and lethal diseases. They blamed disease on the unpredictable acts of the gods, the evil influence of supernatural beings, and even their neighbors and friends in an effort to explain why a certain plague struck them without warning. It did not even occur to them that behaviors such as eating rancid food, drinking contaminated water, or failing to wash their hands were aiding and abetting the true culprits—germs.

In this nineteenth-century painting, the angel of death descends as the plague strikes Rome. In ancient times, the existence of germs was unknown.

Even ancient doctors and others who healed the sick and ministered to other health needs made these mistakes since they were as ignorant about the causes of disease as everyone else. It was not uncommon, for example, for doctors to see dozens of patients each day without ever stopping to wash their hands. This lack of simple hygiene undoubtedly resulted in the spread of various illnesses and countless deaths.

Such was the case with puerperal, or childbed, fever. Doctors unknowingly carried the fever germs on their hands from birthing bed to birthing bed, and one doctor with dirty hands could distribute the disease through an entire village or hospital ward. In this way, the disease spread, killing thousands of women.

Had past societies known that an act as simple as hand washing could slow or halt the spread of some diseases, life might have been very different. Unfortunately, it would take the discovery of germs and their relationship to disease to change people's habits. The confirmation of the germ theory of disease, when it finally came during the 1800s, was nothing short of miraculous. For the first time in human history, scientists realized that people might not be so helpless in the face of disease. Researchers learned that simple hygiene goes a long way toward preventing the growth and spread of many harmful germs. In hospitals, for example, sanitation standards and practices, sometimes as simple as routinely changing and washing bedsheets, were introduced.

Eventually, the confirmation of the germ theory led to other momentous medical discoveries and developments. Among these were antibiotics, new vaccines, and other ways to fight harmful germs as well as new and inventive ways to use harmless germs to improve the human condition, such as in sewage treatment, mining, and cleaning up oil spills.

None of these remarkable developments would have come to pass, however, if not for the curiosity and courage of a few dedicated individuals, the scientists who revealed a fundamental reality that had long remained hidden from humanity. Namely, within the familiar visible world there is another realm—an invisible, seemingly alien world filled with thousands of mysterious microscopic organisms that affect plant, animal, and human life in countless ways.

CHAPTER 1

Early Attempts to Explain Disease

Before people knew about germs, the chances of catching a disease and dying from it were much greater than they are today. No one realized that millions of germs swarmed everywhere—in the air people breathed, the water they drank, the food they ate, the soil they tilled, and even on their own bodies. Dangerous germs passed freely from person to person, from house to house, and from village to village. As a result, periodic outbreaks of crippling or deadly diseases have occurred throughout history. Epidemics of measles, yellow fever, bubonic plague, leprosy, cholera, typhus, smallpox, and other debilitating maladies regularly wiped out thousands or millions of people at a time.

Occasionally a literate person jotted down an eyewitness account of the devastation wrought by such an epidemic, and some of these accounts have survived to the present. The Greek historian Thucydides, for example, recorded the effects of a terrible plague that struck his home city of Athens in 430 B.C.:

> People in perfect health suddenly began to have burning feelings in the head; their eyes became red and inflamed; inside their mouths there was bleeding from the throat and the tongue, and the breath became unnatural and

A Deadly Disease Strikes Athens

Germs have changed the course of history many times. One of the more famous plagues of ancient times was the one that struck Athens in 430 B.C., shortly after the start of the devastating Peloponnesian War, which Athens lost in part because of the epidemic's effects. In his chronicle of the war, the Athenian historian Thucydides describes the malady, which to this day has not been positively identified.

The plague originated, so they say, in Ethiopia in upper Egypt, and spread from there into Egypt itself and Lybia and much of the territory of the King of Persia. In the city of Athens it appeared suddenly.... People in perfect health suddenly began to have burning feelings in the head; their eyes became red and inflamed; inside their mouths there was bleeding from the throat and the tongue, and the breath became unnatural and unpleasant. The next symptoms were sneezing and hoarseness of voice.... Next the stomach was affected with stomach-aches and with vomitings of every kind of bile.... If people survived [for a full eight days], then the dis-ease descended to the bowels, producing violent . . . and uncontrollable diarrhea.... For the disease, first settling in the head, went on to affect every part of the body in turn.... It affected the genitals, the fingers, and the toes; and many of those who recovered lost the use of these members; some, too, went blind. There were some also who, when they first began to get better, suffered from a total loss of memory, not knowing who they were themselves and being unable to recognize their friends.

A modern engraving depicts the disastrous onset of plague in Athens in 430 B.C.

unpleasant. The next symptoms were sneezing and hoarseness of voice.[4]

The death toll was huge—more than 20 percent of Athens' population of about 250,000 perished. Just as demoralizing was the fact that no one knew what caused the disease or how to combat it. There was no choice but to sit back, let it take its course, and hope that one's own household would be spared. Indeed, the horrors associated with such epidemics were generally accepted as facts of life in every culture.

Unsanitary Conditions Bred Disease

Often, however, people were more than simply passive victims who had no way of preventing or lessening the ill effects of epidemics. Unknowingly, they sometimes facilitated the spread of disease and increased the death toll by living in filthy, unsanitary conditions. Many families lived in stone or wooden shacks, with as many as six to ten people living in one or two rooms. Many of these dwellings had cold dirt floors, which turned damp and soggy when it rained. Sleeping and eating areas often became caked with mud from the outside and littered with decaying scraps of food from the inside.

Those who lived in nicer houses with wooden floors were not much better off. They, too, were exposed to the garbage that most people threw into the streets, walkways, and gardens. Germs grew in the rotting garbage, and people and animals then walked on this litter and carried the germs into houses on their shoes or feet. The streets also bore signs of human and animal waste. Some people kept buckets or barrels for such wastes in the house, and when these containers became full, people dumped them into street gutters, backyard manure piles, ponds, and streams. Those with separate outhouses also dumped their accumulated wastes outside in piles. Often, the sun dried the manure into a powder, which the wind blew over villages and houses and into open windows.

Water sources were also common sources of contagion. It was not unusual for all the inhabitants of a village to use a single well or other water source for both washing clothes and drinking. Most people were not careful about keeping the water clean, and it frequently became contaminated by garbage, waste, and other litter. In addition, dogs, pigs, goats, and other animals drank from or walked through the water, contaminating it.

In addition, by today's standards most people were terribly careless in preparing the food they ate. They often slaughtered their animals with dirty knives, then stored the meat in hot, filthy cellars. Few people washed vegetables and fruits before eating them, and it was common practice to eat fruits and vegetables that insects and rodents had nibbled. Refrigeration, which slows the growth of germs, did not yet exist, so food did not keep very long before it spoiled. Vegetables lasted a few days at most, but people kept meat for weeks, sometimes even months. This allowed germs to breed in the spoiled food, and those people who ate it became ill. Another problem was that people often did not thoroughly clean their dishes, cups, and knives after eating, and any remaining crusts of decaying food on these utensils became breeding grounds for disease germs.

The decaying corpses of humans and animals also played a role in the spread of disease. In ancient and medieval times, for instance, it was common practice for people to touch rotting bodies with their bare hands while moving and preparing them for burial. Moreover, sometimes diseased bodies were thrown into lakes or streams, contaminating the water. In these ways, disease traveled from the dead to the living.

An Aversion to Bathing

Personal cleanliness was another problem; for the most part, bathing was not a regular habit before the twentieth century. There were exceptions to this rule. For instance, the noble and wealthy classes in ancient Egypt appear to have bathed frequently and covered their freshly washed bodies with special ointments and deodorants. The Romans, too, placed a great deal of emphasis on cleaning themselves and regularly visited the many public baths found in Roman cities.

In most cultures, however, personal cleanliness was largely neglected and sometimes actually frowned

Erected in the early third century, the baths of Caracalla were among many public bathing facilities in ancient Rome.

on. The thirteenth-century Christian monk Saint Francis of Assisi proclaimed that refusing to bathe was a gesture that proved one's devotion to God, and many people in Europe followed his teachings and never washed. Spain's Queen Isabella, who granted Christopher Columbus his ships, bragged that she had bathed only twice in her life. The first time, she said, was when she was born, the second was just prior to her marriage. In colonial Pennsylvania and Virginia, where nudity was viewed as sinful, there were written laws that banned or strictly limited bathing. One law stated that a person who took a bath more than once a month would be jailed.

Often, being dirty was not just a matter of custom or personal choice. Sometimes it was difficult to find the proper means to keep clean. In medieval and early modern Britain, for example, running water did not exist, streams were freezing or dirty, and soap was scarce and expensive; not surprisingly, lacking easy means of bathing regularly, most people did not develop strong cleanliness habits. The consequences of this general lack of hygiene were sometimes disastrous since the dirtier that people were, the easier it was for germs and disease to spread. Dysentery, childbed fever, and infantile diarrhea killed millions of people in Europe during the nineteenth century alone.

To make matters worse, filthy bodies were, more often than not, infested with bugs; head lice, bedbugs, fleas, and other tiny creatures were unwanted but frequent visitors in most households. More than just irritating pests, these bugs carried deadly diseases. For example, lice often carried relapsing fever, and fleas spread bubonic plague. Infected pests also lived on people's clothes, bed linens, and pets, making it all the more difficult for people to escape the ravages of disease.

Sorcerers, Demons, and Angry Gods

Throughout history, people living in such dismal conditions sought explanations for their misery. But because their scientific knowledge of the world was limited, they did not usually find the right answers to their questions. Early theories about the cause of disease varied from society to society, but most views fell into a few broad categories. One of the

A medieval woodcut shows the fate of a woman supposedly possessed by demons. A common belief held that demons caused disease.

most popular beliefs was that disease was the result of sorcery, or black magic. Those who accepted this supernatural explanation for illness were convinced that sorcerers used magical powers to make people sick. In one nefarious method, the sorcerer first constructed a doll that represented the victim, then stabbed or burned the doll, which supposedly caused the victim to experience pain and distress. The doll could also be painted or manipulated to make it appear diseased, in which case the victim contracted the disease. Another way that sorcerers might hurt someone was to cast a spell over a discarded remnant from the victim, such as a hair, a nail clipping, or a piece of excrement.

In a similar vein, some ancient peoples thought that disease was caused by demons or evil spirits that invaded a person's body. Since most people believed that gods and spirits controlled many aspects of their lives, it was natural for them to assume that such spirits were also responsible for disease. In fact, in many cultures a separate demon existed for each disease. The ancient Mesopotamians, for instance, believed that the demon Askakku caused consumption (tuberculosis). Nergal, another mean spirit, brought fever. The worst illnesses were thought to be inflicted by the so-called evil seven demons of disease. Mesopotamian doctors were so terrified of these creatures that they became superstitious about the number seven and refused to treat a patient on the seventh day of an illness. These "doctors" believed that the only cure for a person possessed by a demon was to exorcise, or chase away, the demon.

Perhaps the most widespread theory of disease was that it was a punishment brought by the gods. In the most primitive societies, sickness was considered the punishment when someone broke the traditional social or religious taboos (accepted rules forbidding people to act in certain ways). Many cultures have taboos against eating certain foods, entering specific areas like forbidden caves or forests, or marrying specific kinds of people. Many ancients believed that breaking such a taboo made the gods angry and the punishment might be the infliction of some terrible disease. The belief in taboos was so strong that those who survived the punishment usually never repeated the infraction a second time.

In many societies, this concept developed into the idea that a god or gods used disease to punish wicked people. If a person or whole family caught a disease, it was often viewed as a sign that someone in the family had angered the gods. And when an epidemic spread through an entire town or country, it meant that God had deemed that place to be corrupt.

Onslaught of the Black Death

The most dramatic example of the belief in disease as a punishment was the terrifying outbreak of bubonic plague that occurred in Europe during the fourteenth century. Also commonly called the Black Death, the plague swept from town to town and from country to country, spreading fear and chaos as well as death. The plague was carried by germs that infested fleas, which passed to rats, which, in turn, brought the contagion to humans.

Bubonic plague afflicts people in the following manner: Once on human skin, the fleas bite and then, prior to feeding, regurgitate (vomit) plague bacteria directly into the tiny open wound. Inside their new host, the bacteria move through the lymphatic system to the lymph nodes and there multiply, forming large colonies. Within three to eight days, the resultant swelling creates the egg-shaped lumps, or buboes, usually in the groin or underarms, that characterize the disease. After another three or four days, the bacteria reach the bloodstream and move to the vital organs, especially the spleen and lungs. This usually leads to dark spots on and then bleeding from the skin, bleeding from the bowels, and in most cases, if untreated, death.

An illustration from a sixteenth-century German book depicts a plague victim showing his doctors a boil under his armpit.

Scholars generally agree about how the bubonic plague epidemic reached Europe and spread throughout the continent. The earliest known appearance of the Black Death in its great mid–fourteenth-century onslaught was in a Christian community just south of Lake Balkhash (in central Asia, about one thousand miles east of the Caspian Sea). Archaeologists have found a cemetery with an unusually high number of graves dating to the years 1338 through 1339; three of the gravestones actually identify plague as the cause of death. This, along with other evidence, suggests that the disease originated somewhere in the vast steppes of central Asia.

During the 1340s the Black Death moved southward into India and also westward along the ancient trade route that ran from the Far East, through the Mongol (or Tartar) lands in what is now southern Russia, to the Black Sea region. By 1345 huge numbers of Mongols in the Russian steppes were dying of the disease. Then it reached the Crimea, a peninsula on the northern shores of the Black Sea, where during the winter of 1345–1346 a Mongol chieftain laid siege to the Genoese colony of Kaffa. (At the time, the Genoese, hailing from Genoa, an independent republic in northwestern Italy, were aggressive traders, whose ships regularly visited ports all along the coasts of the Black and Mediterranean Seas.) During the siege, the Mongols employed a novel and deadly weapon. According to a contemporary Italian account:

> They ordered corpses to be placed in catapults and lobbed into the city in the hope that the intolerable stench would kill everyone inside. What seemed like mountains of dead were thrown into the city, and the Christians could not hide or flee or escape from them, although they dumped as many of the bodies as they could into the sea. . . . One infected man could carry the poison to others, and infect people and places with the disease by look alone. No one knew, or could discover, a means of defense.[5]

After many months of misery, some of the Genoese managed to escape in their ships and sailed toward the Mediterranean. They had no idea that they carried with them a microscopic cargo of death. By 1347 the Black Death had begun to ravage Constantinople, the great Byzantine trading city lying astride the straits connecting the Black and Mediterranean Seas. Because thousands of ships from all over the Mediterranean routinely docked there, it was virtually inevitable that the disease would subsequently spread, via shipping, to the ports of Syria, Palestine, Egypt, northern Africa, Greece, Italy, France, and Spain. And indeed, all of these areas were infected by

No Tears for the Dead

The fourteenth-century Italian literary master Giovanni Boccaccio described the horrors visited by the Black Death on the city of Florence in 1348 in this passage from The Decameron.

> Many ended their lives in the public streets, while many others who died in their homes were discovered dead by their neighbors only by the smell of their decomposing bodies. The city was full of corpses. The dead were usually given the same treatment by their neighbors. . . . They would drag the corpse out of the home and place it in front of the doorstep, where, usually in the morning, quantities of dead bodies could be seen by any passerby. . . . The dead were honored with no tears or candles or funeral mourners; in fact, things had reached such a point that the people who died were cared for as we care for goats today.

early 1348. One Byzantine writer claimed, "A plague attacked almost all the seacoasts of the world and killed most of the people."[6] The horror was that this was only a slight exaggeration. In some cities and regions, as much as half or more of the population died, and only a few areas escaped with a death rate lower than 30 percent.

A Staggering Death Toll

From Europe's ports, the Black Death next raged inland, moving northward and eastward. Describing its terrifying passage through the French countryside, the contemporary French chronicler Jean de Venette recorded:

> Such an enormous number of people died in 1348 and 1349 that nothing like it has been heard or seen or read about. . . . A healthy person who visited the sick hardly ever escaped death. . . . To be brief, in many places not two men remained alive out of twenty. The mortality was so great that, for a considerable period, more than 500 bodies a day were being taken in carts from the Hotel-Dieu [hospital] in Paris for burial in the cemetery of the Holy Innocents.[7]

After the disease had decimated northern France, its trail of destruction reached the English Channel, which, contrary to the hopeful expectations of the English, provided no barrier to the contagion. Late in 1348 the epidemic struck southern Britain with a fury, and by the end of 1349 it had reached the Scottish highlands and eastern Ireland.

At the same time, traders and travelers unwittingly carried the Black Death through what is now Germany and Russia. In 1352 it reached Moscow, where it claimed the lives of the local grand duke and the patriarch of the Russian church, along with untold numbers of less prominent people; then it spread southward and decimated the city of Kiev. Ironically, the lethal contagion had taken a long, cir-

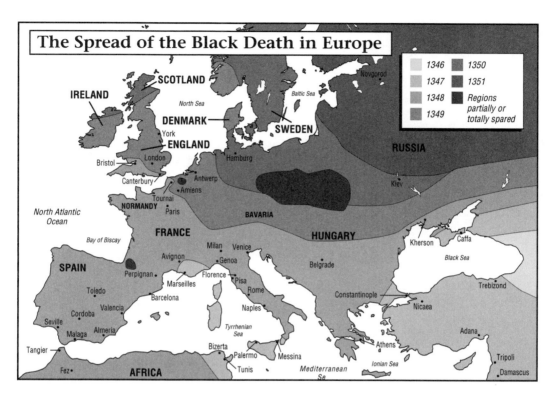

The Spread of the Black Death in Europe

cuitous route to Kiev—southward from the Crimea, through the seas, to southern Europe, and then northeastward into Russia. As noted historian of medieval times David Herlihy puts it, "Launched at Kaffa in the Crimea, and now attaining Kiev, some 700 kilometers to the north, the plague almost closed a deadly noose around Europe."[8]

Modern scholars place the overall casualties for the Black Death at a minimum of 25 million dead, about a third of Europe's total population at the time. Yet that staggering death toll represented only part of the devastation wrought by the Black Death. The disease seemed to kill indiscriminately. Often it wiped out whole families or entire neighborhoods and villages; yet in many other instances, people who had been in close contact with those infected did not contract the pestilence and unaccountably survived. Because no one knew what it was—or, more importantly, how to escape or defend against it—the disease spread an overwhelming fear that frequently eroded the basic bonds of civilized life. According to the medieval Italian writer Giovanni Boccaccio:

> This disaster had struck such fear into the hearts of men and women that brother abandoned brother, uncle abandoned nephew, sister left brother, and very often wife abandoned husband, and—even worse, almost unbelievable—fathers and mothers neglected to tend and care for their children as if they were not their own.[9]

In time, these bonds were reestablished. But the way that Europeans viewed death, God, and life in general had been permanently altered. Why had doctors and especially priests, God's servants on Earth, been unable to stem the plague's hideous tide? Was the disease indeed a punishment inflicted by God to punish humanity's sins? Or did God simply not care what happened to human beings? In his widely acclaimed book about the Black Death, scholar Philip Ziegler states:

> If one were to seek . . . one generalization . . . to catch the mood of the Europeans in the second half of the fourteenth century, it would be that they were enduring a crisis of faith. Assumptions which had been taken for

Punishment for Pride and Corruption

As the Black Death ravaged Europe, no one had any idea what was infecting and killing so many people. Yet there were numerous theories, the most common being that the disaster was a manifestation of God's wrath. An English cleric wrote this tract (quoted in Rosemary Horrox's The Black Death) *as the plague descended on his land in September 1348:*

Terrible is God toward the sons of men and by his command all things are subdued to the rule of his will. Those whom he loves he censures and chastises; that is, he punishes their shameful deeds in various ways during this mortal life so that they might not be condemned eternally. He often allows plagues, miserable famines, conflicts, wars and other forms of suffering to arise, and uses them to terrify and torment men and so drive out their sins. And thus, indeed, the realm of England, because of the growing pride and corruption of its subjects, and their numberless sins . . . is to be oppressed by the pestilence and wretched mortalities of men which have flared up in other regions.

granted for centuries were now in question, the very framework of men's reasoning seemed to be breaking up. And though the Black Death was far from being the only cause, the anguish and disruption which it had inflicted made the greatest single contribution to the disintegration of an age.[10]

Medieval villagers pray to be delivered from the terrors of the plague. The epidemic was thought to be a punishment from God.

The Hidden Realm

Despite this physical and psychological calamity, a few people, mostly doctors and scholars, did not accept the idea that the plague was a divine punishment. They correctly believed that the disease was a natural occurrence. One indication of this was that when people with the plague came into physical contact with healthy people, many of the latter promptly contracted the disease. This led these observers to suspect that the disease spread when "bad vapors" passed from person to person through the air. They thought that disease came from poisonous clouds or appeared when the composition of the atmosphere changed as a result of the influences of various stars and planets. Clearly, although these early men of science did not accept that the plague was a divine punishment and were on the right track with the idea of natural causes, their theories of how the plague and other diseases originated were still blatantly incorrect.

These well-meaning researchers were not alone. Through the ages, doctors, scientists, and scholars tried desperately to understand what caused the various diseases that devastated humanity. But people were severely limited in their discovery of the correct explanation by their lack of technology. The fact is that germs are so tiny that they are invisible to the unaided eye. Advanced medical instruments did not yet exist, and without devices enabling them actually to see germs, people simply had no way of detecting these true agents of disease. Sadly, therefore, for dozens of centuries the microscopic world of germs—a realm literally teeming with life—remained hidden from humanity.

CHAPTER 2

The Modern Discovery of Germs

The discovery and confirmation of the existence of germs in early modern times would not have been possible without the invention of the microscope. It is true that shortly before this instrument appeared a few perceptive individuals made some educated guesses that tiny living things might have something to do with causing disease. During the mid-1500s, for example, as microbiologists Barry E. Zimmerman and David J. Zimmerman point out:

> An Italian physician, Gerolomo Frascatoro, suggested that [the serious disease] syphilis was transmitted sexually by a *contagium vivum*, or "living agent." He outlined the different modes through which these living agents, and those of other diseases as well, could be spread: direct contact with an infected person, handling of contaminated materials, and breathing in infected air. About two hundred years later, in the mid-1700s, the Austrian physician Marcus von Plenciz theorized not only that diseases were caused by invisible living organisms, but also that each disease had its own particular culprit.[11]

Yet although these guesses were basically on the mark, there was no way to confirm them. People had to be able to see germs with their own eyes before they would believe they existed. The trouble was that the human eye cannot detect objects smaller than roughly 1/250 of an inch wide; the majority of disease germs are fifty or more times smaller that that. Clearly, a special instrument that made small things look larger was needed.

No one is certain who made the first microscope. Several Europeans crafted primitive magnifying instruments during the late 1500s and early 1600s. Most of these were simple microscopes that used only one lens. The first person to construct a microscope with two lenses (a compound microscope), which had more magnifying power, was the Dutch eyeglass maker Zacharias Janssen in 1590.

Unfortunately, even early compound microscopes were not powerful enough to reveal organisms as tiny as germs. Furthermore, better microscopes did not develop very quickly because most people regarded the devices as novelties. No one considered microscopes to be instruments useful for serious scientific research. Instead, lens makers and others continued to work with their microscopes as a hobby or to show them off as conversation pieces.

Zacharias Janssen invented the compound microscope. Early versions were not powerful enough to detect germs.

The "Little Beasties"

One of these microscope hobbyists was Antoni van Leeuwenhoek, the owner of a dry-goods shop in Delft, in the Netherlands. In addition to running his store, van Leeuwenhoek also did surveying work and served as Delft's official wine taster. All of these duties left him little time for his hobby of grinding glass into fine polished lenses

Descendants of van Leeuwenhoek's Microscope

The microscope Antoni van Leeuwenhoek used to view germs was a primitive light microscope that magnified images about three hundred times. In this excerpt from their study Microbiology for the Health Sciences, *scientists Gwendolyn R.W. Burton and Paul G. Engelkirk describe the modern descendants of that instrument, explaining how today researchers use lenses of various powers to view some of the larger kinds of germs.*

A single-lens magnifying glass usually magnifies the image of an object from about 3 to 20 times the object's actual size. The light microscope used in laboratories today is a compound . . . microscope with two magnifying-lens systems and a visible light source . . . that passes through the specimen and the lenses to the observer's eye. The eyepiece contains the ocular lens. The second magnifying-lens system is in the objective, which is positioned near the object to be viewed. The two-lens system of the typical compound microscope can magnify 40 to 1000 times. The magnification is usually preceded by an "x" such as "x1000," in which the "x" means "times." The total magnification of a compound microscope is obtained by multiplying the magnifying power of the ocular lens (usually x10) by the magnifying power of the objective lens (usually x4, x10, x40, or x100). Thus, with the low power (x10) objective in place, the total magnification is 10 multiplied by 10 or x100. Usually this objective is used to locate the microorganism to be studied. With the high power . . . x40 lens, the total magnification is 10 times 40, or x400; this lens is used to study algae, protozoa, and other large microorganisms.

Leeuwenhoek demonstrates his microscope to a noblewoman.

and using them as magnifying glasses. Because he could devote only a few hours a week to his lenses, his work progressed extremely slowly during the late 1660s and early 1670s.

Eventually, through the process of much trial and error, van Leeuwenhoek designed and built his own microscopes. The most advanced of these devices could magnify objects three hundred times, making it much more powerful than other microscopes in use at that time. At first, van Leeuwenhoek observed only mundane, everyday objects with his new instrument, including hairs, leaves, salt crystals, the eyes and wings of insects, and even specimens of his own blood. All the while he kept careful notes, describing in detail everything he saw.

To his surprise, in 1673 van Leeuwenhoek noticed what appeared to be tiny creatures swimming in some of the liquids he was studying. He had no idea what these organisms might be, but since they looked and moved more or less like animals, he called them "animacules." At times he also referred to them more humorously as "little beasties." In one of his early descriptions of the animacules, he reported that they were "moving very prettily." Some of them, he continued, were

> a bit bigger, others a bit less, than a blood-globule [drop of blood]; but all [were] of one and the same make. Their bodies were somewhat longer than broad, and their belly,

Germs "A-swimming" in Human Plaque

Among the many letters in which Dutchman Antoni van Leeuwenhoek described his observations of "animacules," what later came to be called germs, was this one (quoted in Clifford Dobell's study of van Leeuwenhoek), reporting his examination of plaque taken from the mouth of a man who had never cleaned his teeth.

While I was talking to an old man (who leads a sober life and never drinks brandy . . .), my eye fell upon his teeth, which were all coated over; so I asked him when he had last cleaned his mouth? And I got the answer that he'd never washed his mouth in all his life. So I took . . . some of the matter that was lodged between and against his teeth [i.e., plaque], and mixing it with his own spit, and also with fair water . . . I found an unbelievably great company of living animacules, a-swimming more nimbly than any I had ever seen up to this time. The biggest sort (whereof there were a great plenty) bent their body into curves in going forward.

which was flatlike, furnished with sundry [various types of] little paws wherewith [with which] they made such a stir in the clear medium . . . that you might even fancy you saw a pissabed [a small insect] running up against a wall. . . . They made a quick motion with their paws, but for all that [effort] they made but slow progress.[12]

As time went on, van Leeuwenhoek noticed the presence of animacules in more and more of the substances he studied. He found them in pond water, food, urine and excrement, and on the bodies of insects; he also saw vast swarms of the mysterious creatures in the scrapings taken from between his own teeth. "For my part," he jotted down in 1683, "I judge . . . that all the people living in our United Netherlands are not as many as the living animals that I carry in my own mouth this very day."[13]

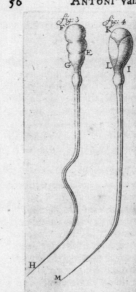

This page from Leeuwenhoek's published observations shows some of his many drawings of sperm cells.

Germs Are Merely a Curiosity

From 1674 until his death in 1723, van Leeuwenhoek wrote long, detailed letters to the Royal Society of London, a respected organization of British scientists. In the letters, he described his microscopic observations, including those of the numerous and strange animacules. He also shared his new knowledge with other European scholars. However, neither he nor any of the other researchers had the slightest idea what the microscopic animals were or where they had originated. They certainly did not associate these tiny creatures with disease.

As far as anyone could tell at the time, these microscopic organisms were perfectly harmless and served no particular purpose. To most scientists, the animacules were merely curiosities, undeserving of costly and time-consuming investigation and study. For more than a century, therefore, the few scientists who did study animacules, which became popularly known as germs during this period, merely catalogued them. The researchers did not offer any important theories about the function germs might serve in nature.

Another reason that knowledge of germs progressed so slowly was the lack of good microscopes. Van Leeuwenhoek's lenses were by far the best of his day, but few people used them. And although he graciously shared most of his discoveries with other scholars, he was very secretive about his work with lenses. He never told anyone about how he ground the glass so perfectly, nor did he reveal the secret process he used to illuminate his specimens under the microscope. This special process was not rediscovered until nearly two centuries later, so few researchers possessed the technology needed to study germs in any detail until the 1800s.

Spontaneous Generation

During the late 1600s and all through the 1700s, scientists continued to believe that germs played no vital role in nature. Still, although there was little or no serious study of germs, the existence of these tiny creatures did cause some members of the scientific community to wonder about their origins. This question rekindled a debate that had been occurring on and off for more than a century. On one side in the debate stood the vast majority of scientists, who believed that life sprang suddenly from nonliving matter, an idea generally referred to as the theory of spontaneous generation. At the time there seemed to be ample evidence for this notion. Maggots appeared to grow spontaneously from decaying meat, for instance. Similarly, the common belief was that rotting wheat produced mice, and toads and snakes were spawned from moist soil and mud.

However, a handful of scientists disagreed with this hypothesis, saying that life could not spring from nonliving materials. Instead, they insisted that all living things must have come from other living things. To rebut their opponents, they argued that maggots appeared in decaying meat because flies had earlier laid eggs in the meat.

Unfortunately, this logical reasoning did not sway the supporters of spontaneous generation. In fact, they contended that the newly discovered existence of germs helped to confirm their own theory; to illus-

Lazzaro Spallanzani was one of a handful of eighteenth-century scientists who rejected the doctrine of spontaneous generation.

trate their point, they conducted a simple experiment. They observed some water under a microscope and noted the germs floating around in the liquid, after which they boiled the water and found that the germs had disappeared. A day or two later, they looked at the water again and saw that it once more swarmed with the tiny organisms. In their opinion, based on these observations, the germs had sprung spontaneously into existence from nothing more than everyday water.

It did not take long for an Italian scientist named Lazzaro Spallanzani to

voice his objections to this conclusion. In 1767 he conducted his own experiment with germs by pouring some chicken broth teeming with them into three flasks. He left one flask open, plugged the second with a porous cork, and sealed the third flask completely by melting the glass together at the top. Then he boiled the broth in each flask, destroying the germs. As he suspected would happen, in a day germs reappeared in the first two flasks, but the one that had been securely sealed remained germ-free.

In Spallanzani's view, the experiment proved that germs had entered the boiled broth in the first flask from the air. Because they were so tiny, the germs also penetrated the porous cork in the second flask. But the air and the germs it carried could not get into the third sealed flask at all, and that was why it was germ-free. Therefore, Spallanzani asserted with confidence, germs did not appear out of nowhere; rather, they simply passed unseen through the air.

Spallanzani's experiment did not end the debate over spontaneous generation, but it did shed some new light on the behavior of germs. Namely, his tests had demonstrated some of the ways in which germs could spread to various materials. Unfortunately, however, most scientists continued to assume that germs, which they began to refer to as microorganisms or microbes, were harmless. They simply saw no indication that the tiny creatures had any effect whatsoever on either living or nonliving things.

Germs Are Linked to Changes in Wine

The discovery that germs *do* bring about changes in other things came quite by accident. In 1854 the well-known French chemist Louis Pasteur received an unusual request. Some French wine makers asked him to find out why their wine was spoiling. The way he approached the problem was simple but ingenious. First, he observed samples of wine, both spoiled and unspoiled, under his microscope. He noticed large

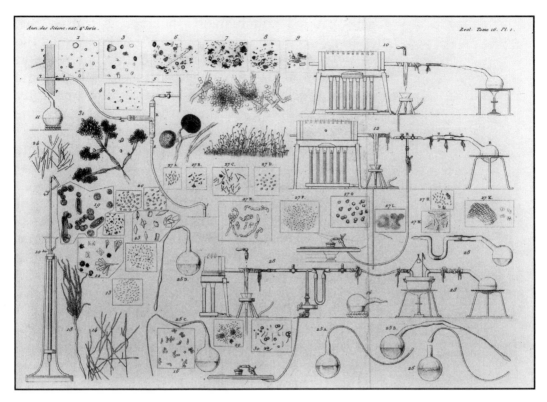

numbers of oval-shaped germs called yeasts in both batches. In the spoiled wine, in addition, he saw large numbers of smaller germs called bacteria, which had been seen many times before. The common belief was that the bacteria sprang into existence as a by-product of the process of fermentation, which changes grape juice into wine.

Pictured is an illustration from Pasteur's groundbreaking scientific paper disproving spontaneous generation.

Suddenly Pasteur had a new idea. Perhaps the bacteria were *not* created during fermentation and maybe they were not harmless, as scientists thought. Furthermore, perhaps it was the yeasts that actually caused the fermentation process itself. To test these assumptions, Pasteur heated mixtures of grape juice and yeasts until the yeasts had been killed. He noted that the grape juice did not change into wine. Yet when he added yeasts to the juice, it fermented in a normal manner.

This proved conclusively that yeasts caused fermentation. Pasteur now observed that as long as the wine stayed sealed, none of the bacteria entered and it did not spoil. Yet when he purposely added some of the bacteria to the wine, the liquid promptly spoiled. In this way, Pasteur showed that some germs cause fermentation and others produce spoilage.

Pasteur solved the spoilage problem in a simple manner. He heated the wine to a temperature that killed the bacteria but not the yeasts and found that the wine retained most of its distinctive flavor yet did not spoil. In his honor, this special heating process became known as pasteurization. A few years later, dairies adopted the idea and began pasteurizing milk in order to remove potentially harmful bacteria.

A Link Between Germs and Disease?

Pasteur's discovery that germs cause fermentation and spoilage created an uproar in the scientific community. He had shown conclusively that germs have specific functions in nature after all. They cause chemical changes in plant juices, and some of these changes are clearly damaging. Other researchers then took the concept a step further and suggested that germs might also do some kind of damage to animals and people. Scientists in several countries began talking about the possibility that germs might actually cause disease.

But there was still a great deal of opposition to this idea in the scientific community. Pasteur realized that it would be difficult to prove beyond question that there was a direct connection between germs and disease; yet he became highly motivated to try. In 1859 his daughter Jeanne died of typhoid fever, inspiring him to work harder than ever to expose the dangers of contact with germs. Pasteur believed that it was possible not only to understand the relationship between germs and disease but also to conquer disease.

Pasteur thought long and hard about how to go about fulfilling these truly formidable goals. And he concluded that his best course was to build directly on his own initial work. His demonstration that germs cause fermentation and spoilage had shown that a link exists between the activity of germs and certain chemical changes in natural substances. Pasteur now attempted to find similar links between germs and disease. He was convinced that bacteria and other types of germs existed by the trillions in the air and soil and on living things and that they somehow reproduced and continued to spread through the environment. Therefore, this process of reproduction might be an important key, he reasoned; understanding how germs reproduce and spread might well lead to ways of controlling them and, by extension, of controlling disease.

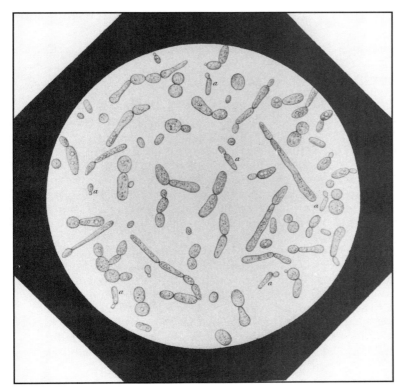

One of Pasteur's sketches of germs as they appeared through his microscope. He was convinced that germs caused disease.

Unfortunately, despite these logical assumptions, which turned out to be correct, Pasteur kept encountering resistance from other scientists. They insisted that germs did not reproduce naturally, as plants and animals did. Instead, opponents of the germ theory kept slavishly falling back on the doctrine of spontaneous generation, declaring that germs just appeared in random places at random times. Because the existence and behavior of germs were random and unpredictable, they could never be controlled, these scientists said.

Pasteur and other supporters of the germ theory finally concluded that in order to be taken seriously in the scientific community, they would have to take the bold step of openly disproving the theory of spontaneous generation. In 1858 a German scientist, Rudolf Virchow, published an official challenge to spontaneous generation, proposing an alternative in its place—the idea of biogenesis, that living cells

How Bacteria Came to Be

Here, from their book Killer Germs, *science writers Barry E. and David J. Zimmerman summarize the likely way that germs, specifically bacteria, first formed on Earth and the tremendous longevity and numbers of these tiny creatures.*

It is likely that, in its early history, Earth's lakes and oceans became a rich organic soup. Water is an ideal medium for molecules to splash around in and react. At some point in the process certain molecules developed the ability to line up amino acids and build proteins to order, and to make copies of themselves, so that the protein-making ability could be passed on. At another point this congregation of super-molecules separated themselves in microdroplets, bound in some way to a membrane, with the internal machinery to take in and use energy and to reproduce. Life on Earth had begun. And the living things were *bacteria*—the most primitive of all cells! For the next *two billion years* bacteria would be the sole inhabitants of Earth, a reign unparalleled by any other living thing. They have persisted twenty-five times longer than the dinosaurs and two thousand times longer than humans. There are more bacteria in a handful of soil or inside your mouth than the total number of people that have ever lived. A single sneeze can carry with it a million bacteria . . . [and] your body contains more bacterial cells than human cells.

could come only from other living cells that already existed. Cells are the basic units of living matter from which all plants and animals are built; according to the theory of biogenesis, germs, which appeared to be one-celled creatures, were produced by other germs. Furthermore, Virchow suggested, cells, including germs, give rise to new versions by dividing in half.

The biogenesis theory also offered an explanation of how germs are related to disease. Virchow argued that disease is not a magic or divine force that takes hold of a body or a body part. Instead, disease begins in the body's cells, where some foreign substance causes cells either to die or to function improperly. Pasteur agreed completely with Virchow and pointed out that germs are tiny enough to infect the cells of plants and animals. Pasteur proposed that germs were almost certainly the disease-causing foreign substances that Virchow had described.

Despite Virchow's efforts, however, the arguments about biogenesis and spontaneous generation continued until 1861. Fed up with a debate that seemed to be going nowhere and impeding important research into the causes of disease, Pasteur set up an experiment designed to show clearly that germs do not arise spontaneously. He repeated the same experiment that Spallanzani had conducted during the 1700s, heating flasks of broth that teemed with germs. But Pasteur's experiment was more carefully controlled than the earlier version, leaving no doubt that germs from the air contaminated the broth and multiplied in it and that germs could travel through the air on dust particles. Moreover, the experiment illustrated another important point. The fact that some flasks remained germ-free showed that germs could be controlled. With this experiment, Pasteur refuted the idea of spontaneous generation once and for all. The way was now clear for serious microbiological research, the final confirmation of the germ theory, and a frontal attack on the microbes that cause disease.

CHAPTER 3

The Germ Theory Proven at Last

During the second half of the nineteenth century, the study of germs became known as microbiology. The period between 1854, when Louis Pasteur showed the relationship between germs and fermentation, and 1914 is now referred to as the golden age of microbiology. During these years, Rudolf Virchow and Pasteur finally laid to rest the antiquated notion of spontaneous generation and proposed biogenesis, the concept that life can come only from other life. In addition, they and other scientists made numerous advances in understanding the different types of germs, their structure, and how they behaved. Finally, and perhaps most important of all, Pasteur and other researchers proved that germs cause certain diseases and demonstrated how some of these diseases spread.

It was during the late 1850s that Pasteur and other scientists set out to prove that germs cause disease. This concept quickly became known as the germ theory of disease. At the time, the germ theory was very hard for most people to accept. This was partly because it refuted traditional explanations, which were often strongly intertwined with widely cherished religious beliefs. For many people, therefore, accepting the germ theory would have meant questioning religious truths and values.

There was another reason for the widespread reluctance to accept the germ theory. Put simply, it did not seem logical. Most people found it extremely hard to believe that invisible creatures could travel through the air and infect plants, animals, and humans. To them, God's wrath seemed a much more believable explanation for disease than germs. Even many scientists refused to accept the idea that such tiny organisms could be responsible for destructive disease.

Lister and Antiseptics

While Pasteur, Virchow, and other scientists struggled to convince these doubters that germs cause disease, a British surgeon named Joseph Lister decided he did not want to wait years for the argument to be resolved. Each and every year, many of his patients died; in his view, even if the germ theory was not yet proven, acting on the mere chance that it might be true might save some of these lives. Lister heard about Pasteur's work during the mid-1860s and agreed that the germ theory made sense. If germs move through the air and fall into broth and wine, Lister reasoned, they might also fall into and infect open wounds.

Lister also remembered what had happened in an Austrian maternity hospital during the late 1840s. A young doctor named Ignaz Semmelweis had been disturbed by the high

Joseph Lister, the brilliant British physician who pioneered antiseptic surgical techniques.

death rate from childbed fever among the women in the hospital's maternity wards. So he studied the doctors' daily routines, looking for clues to the problem. Eventually he noticed that doctors who worked with corpses in one section of the facility often treated women in the wards immediately afterward. Even more noteworthy to Semmelweis was the fact that the doctors did not wash their hands after handling the corpses.

As an experiment, Semmelweis asked the physicians to wash with a chlorine rinse before touching the patients. They did so, and within a few months the incidence of childbed fever in the wards decreased dramatically. Semmelweis did not suspect that germs were involved and had no idea what caused the disease. But his experiment suggested that sanitary techniques could help keep disease from spreading. Unfortunately, most doctors at that time considered the experiment a fluke and the results unreliable, so they made no apologies about continuing to use unsanitary methods.

But Semmelweis's work proved extremely important after all. It influenced Lister, who felt that it supported Pasteur's ideas about germs and disease. If germs did kill people, thought Lister, there was no time to lose. While Pasteur and other scientists searched for proof of the germ theory, millions of people might be dying needlessly. Lister believed that applying some simple sanitary techniques, as Semmelweis had done, might save some lives.

In 1864, at a hospital in Glasgow, Scotland, Lister began using carbolic acid as an antiseptic, or germ-killing agent. He applied a cloth soaked in the acid to wounds caused by serious bone fractures. Normally, nearly half the facility's patients who had such wounds died of a serious infection called gas gangrene. Lister tested the antiseptic for one year, by the end of which the death rate for fracture cases had dropped to 10 percent. This convinced him that germs definitely did

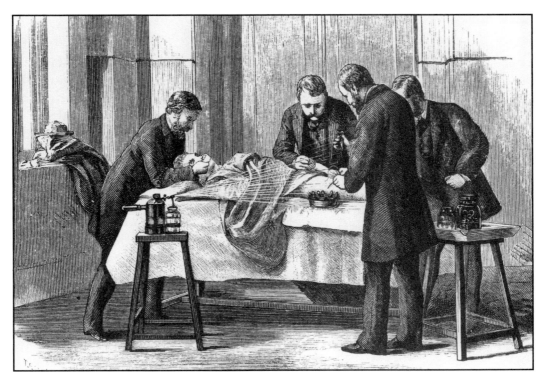

enter wounds through the air. Consequently, he rigged a device that sprayed a germ-killing substance into the air in the hospital's operating rooms. In time, he learned that the risk of infection was far greater from germs on bed linens and human hands than from germs in the air; this prompted him to stop spraying and to introduce in its place strict rules about sterilizing hands, linens, and medical instruments to remove the germs on them.

Unfortunately, most doctors and hospitals were slow in adopting Lister's antiseptic techniques, mainly because there still existed a great deal of skepticism about the germ theory in the medical community. Yet Lister's work did have an important effect on the progress of that theory. Namely, the results of his experiments lent strong support to Pasteur and the other scientists who labored to prove the connection between germs and disease.

A device dispenses carbolic acid spray to kill germs while doctors operate. Lister eventually eliminated the spray and emphasized sterilizing hands and linens.

Koch and Anthrax

One researcher who closely followed the work of Pasteur, Virchow, and Lister was German scientist Robert Koch. Like the others, Koch was convinced that germs cause disease, and he hoped to prove the connection between the two by studying anthrax, a fatal disease that most often strikes cattle, sheep, and other domesticated animals.

Koch had one important advantage over other researchers. One of the problems that early microbiologists regularly encountered was that most germs did not live very long on a microscope slide. Without constant warmth, the germs died before scientists could observe their complete life cycle under magnification. To solve this problem, Koch designed and built a special "warm-stage" microscope that allowed him to keep anthrax bacteria alive for much longer. With this invention, he could view almost the whole reproductive cycle of these organisms under his microscope.

Koch knew that periodic epidemics of anthrax wiped out herds of sheep and cattle throughout Europe. He suspected that germs infected and killed the animals and then entered the soil, where, he reasoned, they managed to stay alive for long periods. Later, according to this view, healthy animals became infected when they came into contact with the germs lying in wait in the soil. Koch believed that this was why the disease tended to remain dormant (inactive) for a while and then later reappeared and killed again.

To test his theory, in his laboratory Koch injected mice and other animals with the blood of sheep that had recently died of anthrax. He found that all of the animals that he injected contracted the disease. He also noted that all the dead animals had a certain kind of rod-shaped bacteria in their blood. Koch was convinced that these were the bacteria that caused the disease. So he placed a sample containing some of the germs under his warm-stage microscope and watched them grow. After several hours, the rods changed, forming a complex tangle of threads, and these threads eventually transformed into tiny spores, or seedlike particles. Koch now needed to answer two key questions. First, did these spores constitute a reproductive stage of the disease? Second, could they infect healthy animals? If the spores did cause the animals to contract anthrax, it would mean that these particles were the agents that transmitted the disease.

Forging ahead, Koch injected some of the spores into lab mice; these mice soon came down with anthrax. He then observed the blood of the mice under his microscope. Instead of spores, there were millions of the rod-shaped bacteria, identical to the ones with which he had started. This proved beyond a doubt that the bacteria reproduced through spores.

The manner in which the anthrax disease cycle worked was now clear to Koch. Bacteria in diseased animals changed into spores, and some of these spores entered the soil. Tough and resistant to extremes in temperature, the spores remained in the soil for months or even years. Thus, the disease would lie dormant until a healthy animal came along and ingested the spores by eating food grown in the soil. Finally, once in the animal's warm blood, the spores sprang to life, reproduced, and the disease spread.

German bacteriologist Robert Koch studies microbes in his lab in this drawing based on a photograph.

Koch firmly established the link between germs and disease in 1876. The global scientific community was quick to accept his findings.

In 1876 Koch presented his findings to German scientists at the University of Breslau. From there, the news traveled all over the world that he had firmly established the connection between germs and disease. In a matter of months, the germ theory became almost universally accepted by scientists. They eagerly voiced their approval of what became known as "Koch's postulates," a set of four statements outlining the basic experimental procedure by which one could prove that a disease had been caused by a certain microbe. Although a few exceptions to Koch's postulates have been discovered since his day, these rules remain an important cornerstone of the methods used in microbiology. The four postulates read,

1. The causative agent [of the disease being studied] must be present in every case of the disease and must not be present in healthy animals.

2. The pathogen [disease-causing agent] must be isolated from the diseased host animal and must be grown in pure culture [in a container in the lab].

3. The same disease must be produced when microbes from the pure culture are inoculated [injected] into healthy susceptible animals.

4. The same pathogen must be recoverable once again from this artificially infected host animal, and it must be able to be grown again in pure culture.[14]

Incredibly, even in the face of such sound, easily-tested logic and laboratory procedure, a few researchers still refused to accept the theory, arguing that anthrax was a disease of animals. Therefore, they said, Koch had shown only that germs could infect and kill animals. These stubborn holdouts insisted that there was still no proof that germs cause human diseases. However, Koch, Pasteur, and their colleagues, confident that the germ theory was well established, ignored these criticisms. The few remaining doubters were silenced in 1882, when Koch discovered the bacteria that cause tuberculosis (TB), a deadly disease that periodically ravages human populations. This finding proved that germs cause disease not only in animals but also in people.

Major Categories of Germs

Scientists realized that by confirming the germ theory they had taken only a tiny step toward a full understanding of the problem of disease. For one thing, there were many different kinds of germs, and researchers knew very little about their various

Pasteur and the Rabies Virus

Even before they could see viruses, some researchers wisely proceeded under the assumption that they did exist. For example, the great French scientist Louis Pasteur was convinced that the disease rabies was caused by a virus and set out to develop a vaccine to combat it. He was unable to find a way to grow the germs in culture, but he discovered that he could produce a constant supply of the disease for study by continually infecting successive generations of laboratory rabbits. After more than four years of experimentation, Pasteur succeeded in making a vaccine for rabies by drying out the spinal cords of rabbits that had died of the illness. Spinal cords that had been dried for one day, he found, contained germs that were still deadly. However, cords dried for fourteen days yielded weakened, harmless rabies germs. Pasteur injected test dogs with several doses of rabies, beginning with the weakest germs and graduating to the more deadly ones. During this series of vaccinations, the dogs gained increased resistance to rabies until they were immune to it. Pasteur repeated the experiment on 125 dogs and none of them contracted the disease. Eventually, he tried the vaccine on a human being—a nine-year-old boy named Joseph Meister, who had been bitten by a rabid dog. Joseph received twelve shots over the course of ten days and subsequently remained free of the disease. With this unqualified triumph, Pasteur had shown that even germs too small to be seen could be conquered.

behaviors. In Koch's and Pasteur's time, scientists recognized four general categories of germs—bacteria, fungi, protozoa, and algae—and there were tens of thousands of different types of germs in each category. Over the course of several decades, researchers proved the existence of a fifth category—viruses—and learned much more about germs in general. Microbiologists found that germs exhibit thousands of different shapes and behaviors and that they are most often single-celled organisms that multiply extremely rapidly.

Bacteria, constituting the first of these categories of germs, are relatively simple and reproduce by dividing in half, a process called fission. They can live in a wide variety of environments and temperatures, some needing oxygen to survive and others able to live without oxygen. Moreover, some bacteria cause diseases, such as cholera, yet many others are harmless and live in and actually benefit the bodies of animals and people.

Some fungi, such as mushrooms, are not germs. It is the microscopic variety of fungi, including the single-celled yeasts, that are referred to as germs. Yeasts are oval-shaped germs and are much larger than bacteria. When yeasts come into contact with certain substances, they cause the process of fermentation to occur, as observed by Pasteur in his famous experiment with wine. Yeasts also cause the decay of dead plant and animal tissue. Some fungal germs reproduce by releasing spores, which spread via wind and water through the environment.

Even larger than yeasts are protozoa, germs with relatively complex internal structures. Protozoa reproduce when their nuclei (central sections) divide, a process called mitosis. Inhabiting water and other liquids, protozoa move almost constantly, propelled by tiny pseudopods, or "false feet." These germs often live inside the bodies of animals or humans and can cause such diseases as malaria and sleeping sickness.

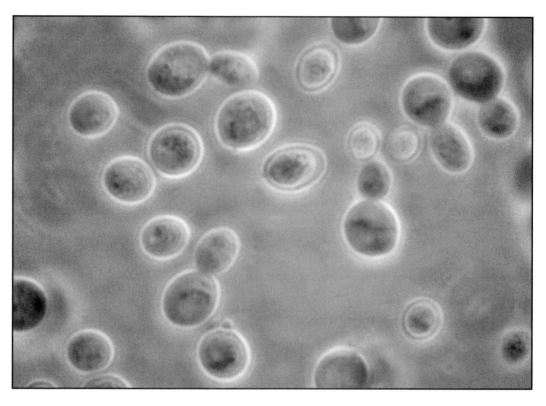

The fourth kind of germ, algae, comes in many shapes and sizes. The most common form, called diatoms, float in vast numbers in the oceans. These organisms contain a green substance known as chlorophyll, which the algae use in photosynthesis, the process in which sunlight and carbon dioxide from the air combine in the presence of chlorophyll to form "food" for the algae. The process also releases oxygen as a by-product. Most of the oxygen in the earth's atmosphere is produced in this manner by ocean algae. Algae are also a food source for larger organisms, such as fish, and therefore form the base of nature's food chain. Most algae do not cause disease.

Viruses, the last category of germs to be discovered, are very different from other kinds of microbes. First, viruses are hundreds and sometimes thousands of times smaller than the others. In fact, viruses are so

Yeasts are single-celled fungi that reproduce by budding, a process illustrated in this photo.

The Origins of Viruses

Several theories have been suggested to account for the origins of the smallest germs— viruses—including the two summarized here by Arno Karlen in Man and Microbes.

One belief is that viruses are degenerated bacteria; they shed every structure save those needed to survive inside a cell (a virus, unlike most bacteria, can survive only within a host cell). Another theory holds that viruses evolved from cellular organelles [small organlike structures inside cells] . . . that escaped to a semi-independent existence. Both ideas have been disputed, but there is wide agreement on the bacterial origin of several types of tiny microbes . . . that were once thought [to be] intermediate between viruses and bacteria, and which cause human diseases such as trachoma and pneumonia.

tiny that they can be seen only with specialized, very powerful microscopes. These organisms are not true cells, as bacteria and other types of germs are. Viruses are tiny corkscrew-shaped strands made up of two simple materials—nucleic acid and protein—and can reproduce only inside of other organisms. Because of this dependence on other living things, these germs are considered to be parasites. While living within a host—the plant, animal, or person they have invaded— viruses can attack the host's cells and cause serious diseases such as smallpox and rabies.

Scientists also learned that viruses tend to adapt to their hosts in order to ensure their own survival, which means that usually only new viruses pose a threat of killing large numbers of people. "The more aggressively a virus reproduces within its host's cells and spreads to new cells," Barry and David Zimmerman explain,

the more rapidly it kills its host. From the virus's point of view, this is not good, for without a host viruses cannot live. A virus would much rather live within an organism and cause that organism little or no harm. This seems to be what the older, more well-established viruses do. Over time and many generations they adapt to their hosts, becoming less virulent [deadly] and allowing their meal tickets to survive. Even the common cold was a deadly killer 5,000 years ago, when it was a recent arrival on the human scene. [Therefore] it is a new virus that wreaks havoc on a population. And, oh what havoc those ill-adapted viruses can wreak. . . . Viruses brought to the New World by Columbus and [Spanish explorer Hernán] Cortes enabled their armies to conquer [the Native Americans who inhabited Central America]. . . . In Mexico City between 1520 and 1522, three to four million Aztecs succumbed to

The Smallpox Virus Ravages the Aztecs

Early European explorers of the Americas carried with them the virus that causes smallpox, which over time killed millions of Indians in North, Central, and South America. Perhaps the worst single example of such carnage was the decimation of millions of Aztec Indians during the early 1500s. Spanish explorer-soldier Hernán Cortés landed at Veracruz (on Mexico's eastern coast) in 1519 and marched a small army to the great Aztec capital of Tenochtitlán (which later became Mexico City). Soon afterward, another Spanish force landed at Veracruz and the two Spanish armies eventually combined into one. At least one person in the second group was carrying smallpox. (The disease had crossed from Europe to the Caribbean island of Hispaniola in 1507, and by 1519 it had killed more than one-third of that island's Native American inhabitants and also spread to Cuba and Puerto Rico.) On June 30–31, 1520, the Spaniards and Aztecs fought a great battle, in which the Indians drove Cortés and his men away from Tenochtitlán. However, among the Spanish dead was the man carrying the disease. Those Indians who handled his body became infected; and they soon infected others. Only a little more than a year later, millions of Aztecs were dead from smallpox, weakening their nation so much that Cortés was able to capture it easily.

This photo taken through a microscope shows cells infected by smallpox.

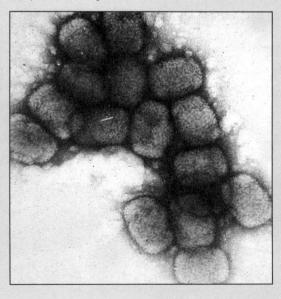

new diseases of the Spanish invaders . . . kill rates running as high as 95 percent in some cities.[15]

Like these deadly viruses, other kinds of germs that cause disease routinely attack the cells of their hosts in one way or another. For example, some germs bore into the cells, damaging them in the process, while others partially digest the cells. Most germs also give off poisons, called toxins, which not only destroy the cells but also travel through the host's bloodstream. Such toxins frequently produce serious physical side effects, such as fever, heart problems, and diarrhea.

Painstaking, Frustrating Work

Because so many different kinds of germs exist, work was slow and difficult for the early scientists who searched diligently for ways to conquer disease. They found that some diseases affected plants only, but others, like anthrax, primarily killed animals. Still other diseases, like the dreaded bubonic plague, killed both animals and people. One of the most significant of these early discoveries was that not all diseases spread the same way. Thus, the distribution of spores, as in the anthrax cycle, was only one of many ways.

Not surprisingly, therefore, the late 1800s and early 1900s became a period of intensive research in the new field of microbiology. It was painstaking, frustrating work since scientists had no choice but to tackle each disease separately. First, they had to find out which germ was involved, then explain the way it attacked the host, and finally, determine how the disease spread from victim to victim. More than two hundred years had passed since Antoni van Leeuwenhoek had first observed germs, yet science had only just begun to uncover the secrets of nature's smallest creatures.

CHAPTER 4

Disease Detectives Track Down Germs

The pioneering work of Louis Pasteur, Rudolf Virchow, Robert Koch, and others firmly established that germs cause disease. This knowledge made it easier to track the spread of disease because now, at least, scientists knew what to look for, even if they did not know exactly where to look. Nevertheless, many challenges lay ahead. More powerful microscopes came into use during the late 1800s, allowing researchers to study germs in increasingly greater detail. Experiments involving germs were conducted in labs in Germany, Great Britain, the United States, Italy, France, and other countries.

The ultimate goal of the scientists and doctors who performed these experiments was to find effective cures for various diseases. But these researchers knew that attaining that goal would be difficult and would take considerable time. Finding out how each disease attacks the body would unquestionably be a slow, methodical process.

These scientists also realized that finding cures for diseases was not the only way to save lives. If people knew how a particular disease spread, the germs that caused that ailment might be controlled. Once Koch revealed that anthrax spores lay dormant in the soil, for example, scientists could easily determine if the spores were present by testing samples of soil from various fields. Cattle at risk could then be moved to spore-free fields where they would be safe from the disease, even if no treatment for anthrax was available.

Tracking the spread of a disease, therefore, was the first step in learning how to control that disease. This is why some of the most important studies about germs and disease in the early days of microbiology took place in outside laboratories. Some researchers went into "the field," which meant that they traveled from town to town, region to region, or country to country, searching for clues about how germs infect people. Not surprisingly, these researchers paid the most attention to those diseases that were the most deadly. Certain killer plagues, for instance, had repeatedly struck large populations throughout recent history, and learning to control these diseases would eliminate much death and suffering.

Urgent Missions to Uganda

Of these epidemic, or rapidly spreading, diseases, sleeping sickness (trypanosomiasis), which repeatedly wiped out entire villages and tribes in many sections of Africa, was long one of the worst. The symptoms of sleeping sickness are unmistakable and devastating. In the first stage of the illness, the victim typically has constant headaches and feels tired and depressed. The person also suffers from insomnia, the inability to sleep. This stage of sleeping sickness often lasts for several months or even a few years. During this time, the victim is unable to function normally and usually becomes a burden on both family and community, which often makes him or her feel useless and even more depressed. In the second stage of the disease, the victim loses the ability to reason and think clearly. Severe pains rack most parts of the body, and the person is constantly drowsy, usually sleeping away much of the day as well as the night.

Eventually, the victim lapses into a coma and, in nearly all cases, dies.

Sleeping sickness, which goes by the local name of *Lumbe* in some parts of Africa, spread to the central African nation of Uganda during the late 1800s. This was a densely populated area, so the disease caused widespread suffering and death. Between 1900 and 1907, some two hundred thousand people died from sleeping sickness in Uganda, and the British, who had administered the country since 1894, were alarmed. British medical personnel worried not only about the huge loss of life but also about the possibility that the disease might spread to Ethiopia, Egypt, and other populated African regions, claiming many more thousands of victims.

For these reasons, the British sent an official medical group—the Sleeping Sickness Commission—to Uganda in 1902. Members of the commission tried to find out how the disease spread by mapping the outbreaks in

Two African children suffer from the insidious sleeping sickness in this late nineteenth-century photo.

A Less-Familiar Protozoan Killer

Sleeping sickness and malaria are perhaps the best-known protozoan diseases and each has caused serious epidemics that have killed thousands of people. Less familiar to the general public but no less deadly is another protozoan disease—leishmaniasis. Spread by a blood-sucking sand fly, it affects hundreds of thousands, and sometimes millions, of people each year. In 1990, for

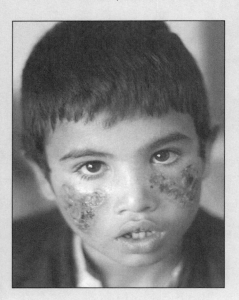

example, some 12 million cases of the illness were reported worldwide. The most lethal form of leishmaniasis is often called *kala-azar*, the symptoms of which include high fever, anemia, enlarged liver and spleen, and a gray hue to the skin. If not treated properly, death can result. The disease kills when the protozoan germs invade the body's white blood cells, which are designed to fight such intruders; the loss of these white blood cells impairs the immune system, which is then unable to fight off other kinds of infection.

A ten-year-old Afghan boy suffers from leishmaniasis in 2002.

specific villages. They were soon intrigued when they found that a definite pattern of infection existed. The disease occurred almost exclusively on lake islands or in villages located on lakeshores and along riverbanks. Conversely, there were no important outbreaks of the sickness in areas far from water. Based on these facts, some of the commission's doctors reasoned that there must be dangerous germs in the water and that people were catching the disease by drinking contaminated water. This explanation seemed quite logical, based on the experiences of one British doctor nearly fifty years earlier in London. That doctor, John Snow, did not know what caused disease since the germ theory had yet to be proven. But through painstaking investigation, he discovered that the source of a series of cholera epidemics was to be found in one of the city's drinking-water pumps.

The doctors with the Sleeping Sickness Commission in Uganda followed Snow's example and initially concluded that contaminated drinking water was the cause of the local epidemic. Unlike Snow, however, the commission's doctors were able to test the water for the presence of disease germs. What they found was puzzling, as their initial examination of the local water found no potentially harmful germs.

In 1903 a second commission arrived in Uganda to study sleeping sickness. This new team of researchers was led by Dr. David Bruce, an army medical officer. Bruce looked at the findings of the first commission and offered a different theory of how the disease spread. In Bruce's view, the doctors found no harmful germs in the water because the disease did not spread through the water itself.

Germs from Infected Flies

Bruce based this idea on his own experience with a different disease. He had recently studied an ailment that killed large numbers of livestock in northern Africa. Over time, he had succeeded in isolating the germ that caused the disease, showing that it was a protozoan that infected tsetse flies, large relatives of ordinary houseflies. When the flies bit an animal, the protozoa entered the creature's bloodstream and infected it. Bruce suspected that sleeping sickness might be spreading among humans in the same manner.

Consequently Bruce ordered a study of tsetse flies and their distribution in various parts of Uganda. The researchers found that the flies bred by laying their eggs in water and that the areas in which the insects bred and lived were exactly the same areas where outbreaks of sleeping sickness had occurred. Encouraged, Bruce examined the flies and found a protozoan parasite called *Trypanosoma*. He exposed laboratory monkeys to tsetse flies infected with this

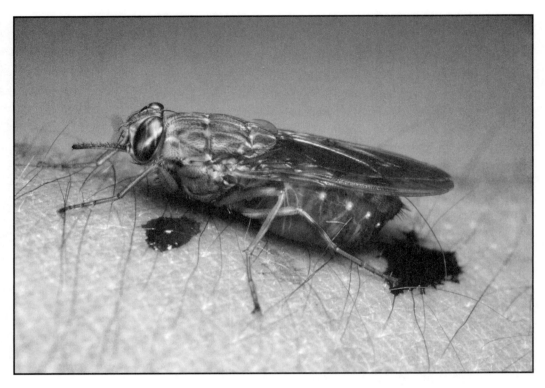

A tsetse fly gorges itself on human blood. Dr. David Bruce proved that the flies often carry sleeping sickness.

parasite, and all of the test animals developed sleeping sickness. Another important piece of evidence emerged when one of Bruce's colleagues, Dr. Aldo Castellani, found trypanosomes in the spinal fluid of human sleeping sickness victims.

Bruce and his team had proved beyond a doubt that sleeping sickness affected human populations living near water because the flies that carried the disease germs could breed only in water. There was still no cure for the disease, but understanding how it spread offered hope that sleeping sickness might be brought under control. In 1907 Hesketh Bell, the British administrator in charge of Uganda, convinced the local chiefs to move their villages away from lakes and rivers. This mass relocation resulted in a rapid and dramatic reduction in the incidence of sleeping sickness in the country. Unfortunately, infected tsetse flies remained. In spite of repeated efforts to wipe out the insects during the twentieth century, the flies continued to spread the disease in isolated areas. Although sleeping sickness no longer wipes out whole villages, deaths from the disease in Africa have been reported as recently as the early 1990s.

The Foundations of Epidemiology

Bruce and his colleagues took the knowledge that germs cause disease into the field and demonstrated one of the many ways that diseases are transmitted and spread through a living population. In doing so, they and other researchers helped to establish some of the basic guidelines and founding principles of the emerging science of epidemiology, the systematic study of disease epidemics. Epidemiologists are, in a real sense, disease detectives who track down clues to the various ways that germs spread disease.

Epidemiologists learned from the beginning that simply explaining how a particular disease spread did not mean that the illness had been beaten, even when a cure was known. This is because new outbreaks of a disease can occur at any time and begin to spread in different, unexpected ways. What makes the examination of these ways easier is knowing exactly what kind of germ to look for; but not knowing the identity of a microbe sometimes sends the epidemiologist down the wrong trails.

Such was the case with influenza, more commonly known as the flu. For many years doctors had a difficult time determining how influenza spread. From their research, they knew that it did not spread through insects, as sleeping sickness did, nor was the flu transmitted to humans by spores or bacteria that grow in unsanitary conditions. What doctors did know all too well was that influenza could be very deadly. Between 1918 and 1919, the disease killed at least 20 million people worldwide. In the United States alone, more than 550,000 people, ten times the number of Americans killed in World War I, died of influenza during that period. The epidemic was so bad that medical officials opened an emergency hospital in Washington, D.C. Dr. James Leake, the head of the facility, remarked, "The only way we could find room for the sick was to have undertakers waiting at the door. . . . The living came in one door and the dead went out the other."[16]

Microbes Spread Through the Air

Efforts at identifying how influenza spread were complicated by the fact that its cause was unknown. Researchers could not see any germs in the bodily fluids of flu victims. Nevertheless, the scientists mistakenly

The Potato Salad Culprit

The methodical, logical way that epidemiologists work is well illustrated in this excerpt from Level 4: Virus Hunters of the CDC, *in which the author, Joseph B. McCormick, a renowned epidemiologist, traveled to Parker, Arizona, to investigate an outbreak of unexplainable sore throats.*

All I was told was that the victims had attended a Fourth of July picnic. . . . An outbreak investigation is very much like the investigation of a crime. It consists of detective work, following hunches, and carefully collecting evidence. In epidemiology, however, the criminal is the bug. Find the bug. And then find how it got into its human hosts. . . . I decided that this investigation needed to be done according to the book—what is called a case control study. This is a scientific method used by epidemiologists to discover the most important differences between those people who did become sick and those who did not. . . . So I

divided people who had been to the picnic into two groups: "cases" (people who had had sore throats) and "controls" (people who had not had sore throats). . . . I set about going from house to house, talking to people, marking my questionnaire, and sticking swabs down people's throats. . . . My case control study allowed me to pick up another crucial clue. All those who became sick had eaten one particular dish at the picnic: potato salad. Now I had to find that potato salad—if there was any left. [He did manage to find it, and] the lab had the final word: the potato salad had harbored the culprit. Definitely strep [throat bacteria]. . . . It appeared that whoever had mixed the salad had been infected with strep. Because this person had not taken adequate food preparation precautions, the strep had gotten into the salad.

assumed that bacteria were the culprits and that they were just too small to see. Based on this assumption, doctors tried tracking and treating the disease with methods that had worked with various bacterial illnesses. But none of these methods worked. The disease did not appear to be caused by fungal or protozoan germs either. It was not until 1933 that scientists discovered that influenza is caused by an altogether different germ—a virus.

This discovery was possible thanks to the invention of special, extremely powerful microscopes, instruments that allowed researchers to detect viruses in bodily fluids for the first time. They were surprised by the revelation that many of the viruses are hundreds of times smaller than other germs. Because scientists found vast numbers of viruses in bodily fluids like mucus and saliva, they concluded that influenza passes from one person to another through the air. When someone coughs, sneezes, or even simply exhales, tiny droplets of saliva and mucus loaded with viruses spray into the air. Other people then breath in the droplets, and the germs enter the bloodstream through the air sacks in the lungs. Disease detectives found that influenza viruses can also pass from people into pigs, ducks, and other animals, which can carry the disease and later transmit it back to humans in a similar manner.

INFLUENZA
FREQUENTLY COMPLICATED WITH
PNEUMONIA
IS PREVALENT AT THIS TIME THROUGHOUT AMERICA.
THIS THEATRE IS CO-OPERATING WITH THE DEPARTMENT OF HEALTH.
YOU MUST DO THE SAME
IF YOU HAVE A COLD AND ARE COUGHING AND SNEEZING. DO NOT ENTER THIS THEATRE
GO HOME AND GO TO BED UNTIL YOU ARE WELL
Coughing, Sneezing or Spitting Will Not Be Permitted In The Theatre. In case you must cough or Sneeze, do so in your own handkerchief, and if the Coughing or Sneezing Persists Leave The Theatre At Once.
This Theatre has agreed to co-operate with the Department Of Health in disseminating the truth about Influenza, and thus serve a great educational purpose.
HELP US TO KEEP CHICAGO THE HEALTHIEST CITY IN THE WORLD
JOHN DILL ROBERTSON
COMMISSIONER OF HEALTH

A sign posted in a Chicago theater during the influenza outbreak of 1918–1919 warns of the contagiousness of the illness.

The Mysterious Philadelphia Killer

One of the more famous successes by modern epidemiologists was identifying a mysterious disease that struck the city of Philadelphia during the 1970s, as summarized here by Arno Karlen in his popular book Man and Microbes.

When a severe respiratory epidemic broke out in Philadelphia in 1976, it was first feared to be swine flu. Many of the victims were American Legionnaires attending a bicentennial-year convention there; hundreds fell ill and dozens died. Yet no flu virus was found, nor was any other familiar microbe.

The mysterious ailment, dubbed Legionnaires' disease, had prominent press coverage for almost six months as researchers sought its cause. They finally found it, a peculiar bacterium that manages to thrive in air conditioners, cooling towers, whirlpool baths, and other places hostile to most life forms. Legionellosis still occurs around the world, especially in hospitals and hotels, and recently on a luxury cruise ship. There may be as many as 50,000 cases a year in the United States alone.

Although scientists had discovered the cause of influenza, epidemiologists found that tracking the disease was still difficult. The problem was that the influenza virus seemed capable of changing its form. So sometimes the disease detectives were not sure if they were dealing with one disease or several similar diseases. Eventually, they learned that viruses could mutate (change) easily, forming new strains of diseases. The main impediment to victims and doctors alike is that a new strain may be resistant to medicines that were effective against a former strain. This had been the case with influenza. It keeps returning; and each time it does, medical experts must develop new medicines to combat it.

Researchers and doctors must also be on the alert for the possibility that a mutated form of the disease might begin spreading in a completely different way. One expert who worries about this possibility is Alan Kendal, formerly of the Centers for Disease Control in Atlanta, Georgia. "Believe me," he states, "we have every reason to be afraid of this virus. Every year it claims thousands of lives in the U.S. When a new strain appears, hundreds of thousands of people may die around the world." Kendal readily admits that scientists still know relatively little about flu viruses. "We don't know what made [the 1918 outbreak] so deadly," he says. "And there is always the chance that another one will strike."[17]

A Modern Disease Detective at Work

If and when such a serious epidemic does strike, the disease detectives stand ready to investigate it and hopefully slow its progress significantly. They use many of the same basic methods their predecessors used, despite the fact that knowledge of germs greatly increased during the twentieth century. The primary tool of epidemiology remains good old-fashioned field work.

Following this tried-and-true tradition, epidemiologist Nathan Shaffer set out in 1987 to help doctors in the small African nation of Guinea-Bissau stop a massive outbreak of cholera. Since the time of John Snow, cholera had continued to plague humanity, with serious epidemics sweeping large areas of the globe in 1899, 1923, and then again during the 1970s. In 1978 alone, seventy-five thousand people worldwide died of cholera.

With this sober reality in mind, Shaffer immediately began his detective work. He first needed to find out how the disease was infecting people, both on the seacoast and in the inland areas. He knew that cholera often spreads through contaminated water. "But," he explains, "the outbreaks didn't seem to be associated with particular wells. . . . The epidemic was spreading up and down the coast. Right away I suspected shellfish."[18] The reason he considered the possibility that shellfish were the culprit was that he knew they often carry waterborne diseases.

Shaffer dutifully went from house to house, asking people how and when they became ill and what they ate as well as questions about their everyday hygiene.

He also tested shellfish from local markets, and he found that the fish did indeed contain cholera bacteria. This explained how the people on the coast had contracted the disease. However, eighty people had died from cholera in an inland village. Puzzled, Shaffer traveled to the village and found that none of the victims had eaten shellfish from the coast.

Faced with a genuine mystery, Shaffer searched for clues and soon learned that one of the villagers had been a dockworker on the coast. The man had recently died of cholera, and his body had been shipped home to the village. Shaffer then discovered that some of the same people who had handled the body during the man's burial had also helped to prepare the funeral feast. Investigating further, the epidemiologist found that more than half of the people who

Epidemiologist Nathan Shaffer gathers a water sample from an African lake. He uncovered the trail of a 1987 cholera outbreak there.

Epidemiologists take soil samples in hopes of finding microbes that will be clues to the spread of a deadly disease.

had attended the feast had contracted cholera. In this way—by asking questions, diligently following leads, and applying simple logic and some creative thinking—Shaffer uncovered the trail the disease had taken in its assault on the local population.

Disease detectives like Shaffer realize that they must always be prepared to fight new outbreaks of diseases such as cholera. In 1991, in fact, Peru and some other South American nations fought a new and dangerous cholera epidemic. As one writer said of the disease, "It remains hovering in the wings like some sinister shadow, ever patient, awaiting its chance once again to carry death abroad in the world."[19]

Scientists and doctors realize that diseases like sleeping sickness, influenza, and cholera will affect humanity for a long time to come. Other dangerous ailments currently threatening humanity include AIDS, hepatitis, Ebola virus, Dengue fever, and West Nile virus. One important way to combat the germs that cause these plagues is to control and inhibit their spread. Some methods might include destroying disease-carrying insects, instituting better sanitation methods, being more careful about eating certain foods, and isolating infected individuals from others. Moreover, modern disease detectives must continue to identify the ways in which potentially dangerous microbes move through the environment and infect plants and animals. Someday, human beings may win the war against the more deadly germs. Until that day comes, people must continue to fight back and win one battle at a time.

CHAPTER 5

A Host of Beneficial Germs

Because humanity is constantly threatened by so many old and new diseases caused by dangerous germs, it is easy to forget that not all microbes are either dangerous or destructive. During the golden age of microbiology, while scientists studied harmful germs, it became increasingly clear that a good many germs are relatively or completely harmless. In fact, researchers discovered that only a small fraction of the germs known to exist in nature cause disease. The vast majority have no effect on or are actually beneficial in one way or another to plants, animals, and humans. Moreover, scientists have established that, without certain kinds of germs, higher forms of life could not exist.

Germs Aid Nature's Cycles

Humans and other higher life-forms have always lived with and today continue to coexist with an abundance of harmless or beneficial germs at every conceivable turn. Indeed, the great Louis Pasteur had been correct in his assertion that microbes exist everywhere in the environment. In countless numbers they float through the air on dust particles, swim through the oceans, and permeate the soil, sewage, and

The Role of Germs in Nature's Food Chain

The food chain begins in the ocean, where microscopic plants such as algae consume sunlight and carbon dioxide from the air and nutrients from the water. Tiny animals, such as zooplankton, then eat the algae. These tiny animals subsequently become food for larger animals such as fish. Humans and other creatures then eat the fish. The waste products of all these creatures are broken down by germs such as fungi and bacteria. In their turn, the broken-down wastes become food for other animals, and the cycle begins again.

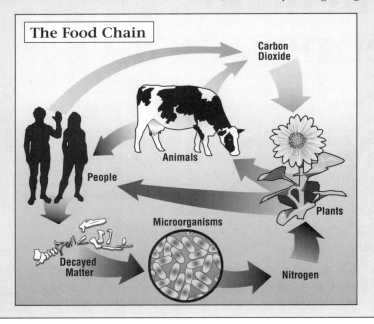

practically every other possible niche on the planet. Germs have even been found in such inhospitable places as frozen Antarctic wastelands and boiling hot springs.

Over time, most of these microbes have become part of the earth's natural cycles. They are involved in the processes that nurture life as well as the processes of decay, which regularly make room for new growth. For example, certain types of germs in the soil help plants consume nitrogen from the air; without nitrogen, plants cannot live, and without plants, many animals cannot live. Because human beings eat both plants and animals, they also depend on the germs that help plants process nitrogen from the air.

Microbes also aid in supplying most of the oxygen that animals and humans take in with each and every breath. Through the process of photosynthesis, ocean algae take in carbon dioxide and give off oxygen. Algae are also important because they form the base of nature's food chain, in which tiny animals eat the algae and then are themselves consumed by larger animals. Eventually, humans (except for strict vegetarians, of course) eat some of these animals, which means that most people indirectly depend on the algae for food.

Still other types of germs live by consuming the tissues of dead plants and animals. In this process, germs release chemicals that cause dead things to decay. And as the dead tissues are broken down into simpler substances, these compounds are recycled back into the environment for use and reuse by living plants and animals. As microbes break down dead tissues, for example, they release elements such as carbon, nitrogen, and phosphorus into the air and soil. Plants take in these vital elements and use them to build their own tissues. Animals then consume the plants, and when these living things eventually die, the process repeats itself over and over. (It is likely,

Germs that Digest Grass

One part of the many natural cycles in which germs play a key role is the process by which cows and sheep digest grass and produce methane and carbon dioxide gas, explained here by microbiologist John Postgate in his book Microbes and Man.

Ruminant mammals, such as sheep and cattle, have a primary stomach (called the rumen), in which grass, which is almost the only food they eat, quietly ferments. The rumen is a sort of continuous culture of anaerobic microbes, including protozoa and bacteria, which collec-

tively ferment the starch and cellulose of grass to yield fatty acids, methane, and carbon dioxide. Rumen juice is extremely rich in microbes . . . and they are very active. An ordinary cow produces 150 to 200 liters [39 to 52 gallons] of [methane and carbon dioxide] gas a day and a large, well-fed, lactating cow is almost a walking gasworks at 500 liters [130 gallons] a day. (The gas, by the way, emerges from the mouth, as a belch, not from the rear end.)

therefore, that every single atom making up the body of a person alive today has been part of the body of a number of other living things that existed hundreds, thousands, and even millions of years ago.) These are only some of the ways that germs help sustain the earth's natural cycles. Pasteur recognized the importance of these beneficial germs when he said, "Life would not be possible in the absence of microbes."[20]

Bodies Covered in Germs

With so many germs in the air, soil, and water, it comes as no surprise that microbes exist on people, too. In fact, at any given moment a clean, healthy person has literally trillions of harmless germs on both the inside and outside of his or her body. Put into slightly more specific terms, microbiologists estimate that there are about 30 million germs on an area of human skin the size of a postage stamp. And even more germs inhabit the inside of the body. In its dark recesses, more than 1 billion microbes can exist in a volume of space no bigger than a kernel of corn!

Unlike disease germs, which attack and damage the body's cells and tissues, the beneficial germs that live in and on the body help to keep it running properly. The harmless varieties of germs live in cavities such as the mouth and rectum, in the intestines, and in the open spaces between the organs. Most of these tiny creatures take advantage of the warmth, moisture, and nutrients available within

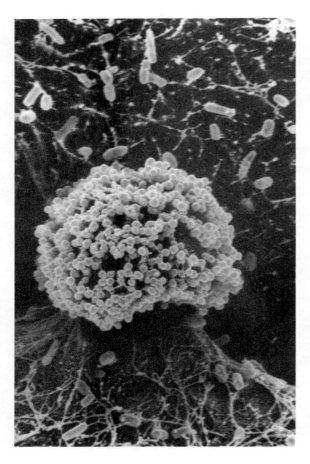

A cluster of bacteria, photographed through an electron microscope. The human body hosts billions of harmless or beneficial bacteria.

an average human body. They subsist by consuming substances that people customarily consider "yucky," including mucus, excrement and other waste products, and dead cells routinely cast off by body parts. Additionally, these germs have become very specialized, with specific kinds living only in specific areas and niches of the body. Indeed, some of these microbes are so specialized that they cannot grow and thrive anywhere else in nature but in a human body.

Research indicates that, just as some germs cannot live without people, people cannot live without some germs. One way that microbes help the body function properly is by stimulating the immune system, the purpose of which is to fight infection and disease. All animals, including humans, have special cells that produce substances called antibodies. These are like tiny soldiers that attack and destroy harmful germs that penetrate the body's tissues. In a way that scientists still do not fully understand, useful germs stimulate the body to produce sufficient antibodies, which means that a person's body relies on its good germs to help defeat invading bad germs.

By conducting experiments with animals specially raised in germ-free environments, scientists have shown that good germs stimulate the immune system. These animals have never been exposed to either good germs or harmful ones, and consequently their immune systems do not function properly. The cells that make antibodies do not develop normally and therefore produce very few antibodies. As a result, the tissues and organs of these animals are wide open to attack by harmful disease germs.

Germs and Humans: A Symbiotic Relationship

Other beneficial germs make it possible for animals and people to digest food properly. The microbes do this by ensuring that the intestines, the long, folded tubes located in the lower abdomen, develop in a

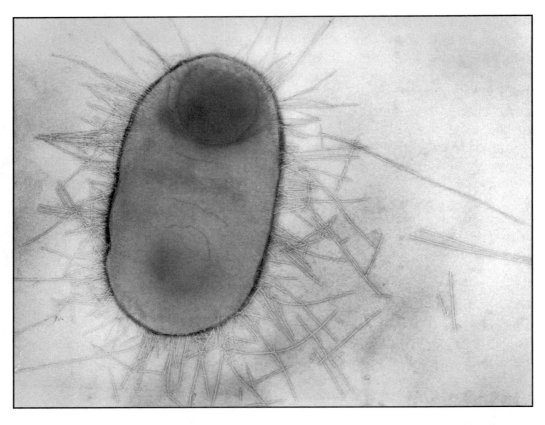

Millions of E. coli *bacteria, like this one, magnified 8,000 times, exist in a normal human intestine.*

normal, healthy manner. After food is partially digested in the stomach, it passes into the intestines; there, further digestion takes place and the nutrients in the food pass into the bloodstream. To work efficiently, the walls of the intestines must be of a certain thickness, and the muscles on the insides of the tubes must be strong enough to contract and push the food along.

Scientists do not know exactly how germs ensure normal intestinal development, but several experiments have suggested that they do play an important role. In these experiments, the researchers raised guinea pigs and other lab animals in completely germ-free environments and found that the intestines of these animals did not grow and develop normally. Specifically, the walls of the upper intestines were too thin and the intestinal muscles were too weak to move the food along in a healthy manner. Eventually, the animals died because their bodies could not absorb sufficient nutrients. Then, the researchers repeated the experiment, this time feeding intestinal bacteria to another group of germ-free guinea pigs. Within a few weeks the intestines of the animals grew thicker and stronger, and the guinea pigs began to digest their food normally. These experiments show that certain kinds of highly specialized bacteria somehow induce the intestinal walls to grow to the proper thickness.

Germs also affect the manner in which the heart pumps blood. The heart must pump a certain volume of blood each minute in order to keep fresh blood moving to the various parts of the body. Experiments have shown that the hearts of germ-free test animals pump a smaller volume of blood than do the hearts of animals containing normal levels of germs. Scientists are still not sure why or how this happens. But they confirm that the presence of microbes in the body is absolutely essential to healthy blood circulation.

Still another way that germs benefit living things is by producing many of the vitamins essential to good health. Certain germs in the intestines take in nutrients from food and chemically transform them into complex vitamins. Without these vitamins made by germs, people would be weak and unhealthy. The vital importance of these germs is revealed by what happens to people who are treated with drugs intended to stop infections. Such drugs often kill large numbers of intestinal germs that normally make B vitamins. These vitamins are essential in breaking down important acids in the body as well as in the production of red blood cells, which carry oxygen throughout the body. Until the internal populations of germs that make B vitamins are restored, these processes slow down, making the patients feel weak and uncomfortable.

All of these examples illustrate that useful germs and human beings enjoy a symbiotic relationship, one in which two living things benefit from living together and sharing many essential resources. The fact that the human body does not develop or function properly without the presence of various kinds of germs is significant; it suggests that as humans evolved and the body developed its present form over the course of millions of years, germs evolved with them. This means that useful, beneficial germs must have been present in the bodies of the most primitive ancestors of today's animals and people. Without microbes, therefore, animals would not have evolved in the same way, and human beings, at least as they exist today, might never have evolved at all.

Germs in Yogurt, Cheese, Beer, and Other Foods

In addition to living in and on people, germs are also found in the foods people eat. Some of these microbes harmlessly multiply on plant and animal products and later enter human digestive tracts when people eat these products. Many important foods are actually produced with the aid of germs, constituting another way that a number of microbes have proved highly beneficial to people.

A variety of dairy products are made with germs, for instance. These products take advantage of the fact that certain germs cause milk to spoil, a process that occurs when bacteria such as *Lactobacillus* attack the proteins, fats, and carbohydrates in milk. The milk sours and acquires a lumpy consistency called curd. When a carton of milk in the refrigerator sours, most people assume that the milk has gone bad and proceed to pour it down the drain. But certain kinds of milk spoilage—including curd—sometimes significantly aid in the production of dairy foods.

Buttermilk is a well-known example of a dairy product that depends on the presence of microbes. Buttermilk is made by adding cultures (colonies of microbes grown in a lab) of bacteria to vats of pasteurized milk. These bacteria cause the milk to ferment, just as yeasts cause grape juice to ferment into wine. When the fermented milk is sour enough, it is ready to be packaged as buttermilk and shipped to stores. A few extra steps in the same process produce a thicker product popularly known as sour cream.

This worker in a dairy facility in Iceland is making a thick milk curd by mixing skim milk with bacteria cultures.

Yogurt is another dairy product made with germs. The first step in preparing yogurt is to boil the milk until it becomes thick like custard. Next, cultures of *Lactobacillus* and other kinds of bacteria are added and the milk sours, just as it does when it gets old in the refrigerator. Finally, the product undergoes evaporation to remove some of the water content and thicken it further; the end product, of course, is yogurt, one of the most popular foods on the market.

Another widely popular dairy product made with germs is cheese. The curd that forms when milk spoils is essentially an unripened form of cheese. Various forms of this curd are sold as cottage cheese, ricotta, and cream cheese, and ripened cheeses, such as Swiss, Romano, and cheddar, are also forms of the curds of spoiled milk. The curds are generally pressed and salted, the salt providing added taste and also keeping the curds from molding. Next, the curds are cut into the desired shape, and certain bacteria are added. Then the cheese is allowed to ripen for several months, during which time the bacteria release acids that give the various cheeses their distinctive flavors.

Bread making is still another example of how germs assist in food production. Most breads are made with yeasts, which ferment the sugars in the bread dough, a chemical process that produces carbon dioxide gas as a by-product. Later, in the oven, heat causes the gas to expand, forcing the bread to rise. (When yeasts are left out of the process, no fermentation takes place and the bread does not rise; the result is unleavened bread, which is flat.)

Caution Against Cross-Contamination

The germs used in producing foods such as yogurt, buttermilk, cheese, and beer are basically harmless. However, people who regularly work with food must be careful not to allow potentially harmful germs to mix with the harmless ones, through handling or other means, as explained by the American Council on Science and Health in their pamplet entitled Eating Safely: Avoiding Foodborne Illness.

"Handling" includes anything that happens to food from harvesting until the food is eaten. Harvest or slaughter, processing, storage, distribution, retailing, final preparation, and serving—all offer chances for contamination, the introduction of disease agents. . . . It is important that surfaces and utensils that have been in contact with raw meat and poultry not be used in handling cooked meats or other foods that will not be cooked before they are eaten unless they have been suitably cleaned. Even the liquid that drops from raw meat or poultry can get onto other foods or food-contact surfaces, resulting in "cross-contamination." People are another important source of food contamination. Infected people who handle food can introduce infectious microbes into or onto the product. . . . An important precaution to prevent contamination of food with infectious agents from humans is thorough hand-washing after toilet use— especially after defecation. This applies to anyone who handles food, but particularly to those who do final preparation and serving, because any microorganism introduced at that late stage is likely still to be alive and infectious when the food is eaten.

In contrast, beer and ale brewers employ yeasts in a different but no less productive way. These beverages are made from grain starches, which the germs have a certain amount of trouble breaking down. So brewers begin by allowing the grains to sprout. Then they dry the grains and grind them into a product called malt, which contains substances that break down the starches. When yeasts are added, the malt ferments, producing beer.

Grape juice ferments in a large vat in a French winery. Some of the wine will be exposed to the air, producing vinegar.

Yeast fermentation is also the process behind another common liquid food product—vinegar. To make vinegar, wine is purposely exposed to the air, and the oxygen in the air causes a chemical reaction in the wine that changes most of the alcohol present to acetic acid. Therefore, vinegar is basically sour wine containing little or no alcohol.

Many other foods are produced by using bacteria to cause fermentation. These include sauerkraut, pickles, olives, vanilla, and soy sauce. In the production of soy sauce, for example, soy beans and wheat are mixed together, crushed, and then cooked. Special bacterial cultures are then added and the mixture is allowed to ferment.

The examples cited illustrate that germs in the oceans, the soil, and in and on animals and people are essential elements of the natural environment. Without these germs, the world would not work the way it does. Human beings have learned to use some of these germs to their advantage, as in the case of bacterial and yeast cultures aiding in food production. Unfortunately, people have also learned to use germs for more destructive purposes, especially warfare.

CHAPTER 6

Germs as Weapons: Biological Warfare

All through the twentieth century, scientists and doctors labored to find ways of fighting the germs that cause fatal diseases. Their goal was to stop the spread of disease. But a few scientists had a completely different and more sinister goal, namely to find ways of inflicting disease on their country's enemies. The idea is a simple one. Since disease germs can kill, they can be used as a weapon if they can be harnessed. This use of germs is known as germ warfare or biological warfare, the latter referring to the fact that germs are biological agents.

Biological warfare has never been used on a large scale. But germs have been used purposely to kill people, animals, and crops in numerous isolated incidents. Many of these events occurred in modern times, although earlier societies also used germs to kill people. The difference between then and now is that we know today how and why germs kill. Ancient people did not. They only knew that they could weaken or wipe out their enemies by spreading disease.

Using Plague and Smallpox to Kill

Indeed, although the ancients did not know that germs cause disease, they knew by simple observation that disease often spread through physical contact. So people sometimes put the diseased corpses of animals and humans in wells and other sources of drinking water to contaminate the water and kill their enemies. Another common tactic was to hurl diseased bodies into walled forts and cities that were under siege, hoping the bodies would spread the disease. This occurred in 1347 during the siege of the Italian colony of Kaffa, located on the northern coast of the Black Sea. The colony was under siege by the Mongols, who catapulted bodies of bubonic plague victims into the city. Thousands of people contracted the plague, and the Italians surrendered. The incident

A priest administers last rites to an Italian plague victim. The Italian colony of Kaffa fell when the Mongols catapulted plague victims into the city.

also had catastrophic consequences for millions of people in distant lands, for after the fall of Kaffa Italian ships carried the plague back to Europe, where the disease wiped out one-third of the continent's population. The very same technique was employed in 1710 when a unit of the Russian army was besieging a Swedish town and hurled plague-infected corpses inside. Many people died, and the town had to surrender.

Smallpox is another deadly malady that has been used as a weapon, perhaps most maliciously against the Indians of North America during the centuries of European colonization. During the Indian wars of the 1700s, for example, Jeffrey Amherst, the commander of British forces in North America, ordered that unwashed blankets that had been used by smallpox victims be given to Indians in the American colonies. As a result, thousands of Native Americans contracted the disease, for which their immune systems had no resistance whatsoever, and died.

Early Biological Weapons Programs

During the late 1800s and early 1900s, as serious experimental work in microbiology progressed, many scientists and government officials recognized the potential of germs as weapons. The use of such weapons was and still is generally considered inhumane. For this reason, government-sponsored research into biological weapons was kept secret; it is sometimes difficult to say with absolute certainty which countries were doing the research and which were not.

The Germans had the most advanced germ research labs at the time, and many experts suspected them of working on biological weapons. During the early 1900s, officials in the United States and Great Britain accused the Germans of developing biological weapons. The Germans denied these accusations. Then, during World War I, rumors spread that the Germans had infected horses with anthrax, a serious disease that usually strikes cattle and other animals, and glanders, a respiratory tract infection of horses and mules. According to British and French informants, the German researchers let the horses loose in France, hoping they would spread the disease to French animals. These rumors were never confirmed. However, it appears certain that the Germans used anthrax to infect sheep that were destined for export to Russia.

By the early 1920s, officials in many countries were concerned about the possible development of biological weapons. Such weapons had the potential to infect millions of people with incurable diseases. Great Britain's Winston Churchill had heard reports of biological weapons research going on in many countries. In 1925, he worried about what he called

> pestilences [contagious diseases] methodically prepared and deliberately launched upon man and beast . . . blight to destroy crops, anthrax to slay horses and cattle, plague to poison not only armies but whole districts—such are the lines along which military science is remorselessly advancing.[21]

Symptoms of Skin Anthrax

Anthrax has often been the preferred disease of biological weapons producers. In this excerpt from her informative book Anthrax: An Investigation of a Deadly Outbreak, *Boston College scholar Jeanne Guillemin lists the symptoms as they would appear in those human cases in which the skin becomes infected.*

In humans, an anthrax infection can begin in one of three ways. Infection through the skin (cutaneous anthrax) is . . . the most common and obvious form. It begins with a tiny pimple. In a few hours this eruption becomes a reddish-brown irritation and swelling that turns into an ulcer . . . that splits the skin. The black scablike crust that the lesion develops gives the disease its name, *anthracis*, the Latin transliteration of the Greek word for coal. . . . Without treatment, the fatality rate for cutaneous anthrax can be 20 percent. In [the twentieth] century, sulfamides, penicillin, tetracycline, and other relatively accessible drugs have reduced fatality to 5 percent or less.

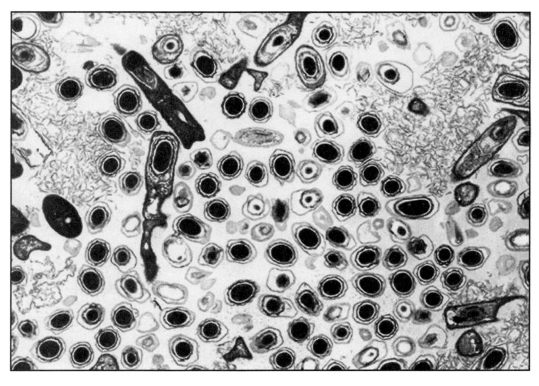

This Department of Defense photo shows anthrax spores, only a few of which can cause a person to contract the disease.

Churchill's reference to anthrax was significant. Scientists and government leaders knew that the disease could kill people as well as animals. People who handled contaminated animals often got skin ulcers and blood poisoning, and there were cases of humans inhaling the bacteria, developing choking coughs and fevers, and then dying. Because of its potential to kill large numbers of people quickly, as time went on more and more of the resources of biological weapons research concentrated on anthrax. According to Boston College scholar Jeanne Guillemin:

> The potential of anthrax as a biological weapon has focused national and international attention on its lethality for humans. Anthrax spores, tough enough to withstand bomb detonation and small enough to aerosolize [transform into a spray or mist], have been the preferred agent for every nation that has sought to develop and produce biological weapons.[22]

Indeed, Churchill was aware that government intelligence reports prepared by various countries during the 1920s indicated that much of the secret biological weapons research being done around the world at that time involved anthrax.

Because of these fears, a clause about germ weapons was included in the 1925 Geneva Protocol, an international treaty opposing the use of weapons of mass destruction. (The full name of the treaty was the Geneva Protocol for the Prohibition of the Use in War of Asphyxiating, Poisonous, or Other Gases and Bacteriological Methods of Warfare; no reference was made to nuclear weapons because their invention was still several years away.) Although no countries at the time admitted to having the "bacteriological methods of warfare" mentioned in the treaty, several nations, including the United States, refused to sign the protocol, mainly because they did not want to risk worldwide condemnation if and when they felt they needed to use such weapons. (The United States finally ratified it in 1974.)

Unfortunately, the Geneva Protocol ended up *en*couraging rather than *dis*couraging research into biological weapons. First, the treaty banned only the *use* of such devices; there was no prohibition against continued research and development and no provision for international inspections. Also, the signing of the treaty by many nations led some governments to suspect that the research was more widespread than previously thought. Fearing that his country might be left out, a Japanese army major named Shiro Ishii toured many of the European microbiology labs and other scientific facilities. He became convinced that his country would benefit from the use of germs as a weapon. In 1935 Ishii persuaded the Japanese government to begin a secret biological weapons program, with the deceptively harmless title "Unit 731."

Humans Used as Guinea Pigs

By 1939 the masterminds of Japan's Unit 731 project had completed the world's first biological warfare installation. It was located in a remote area of Manchuria, which the Japanese had recently taken from the Chinese and now occupied. Some three thousand scientists and technicians worked at the top-secret complex, which had its own school, hospital, air base, and other facilities, making it a self-contained and self-support- ing community. The deadly or disabling diseases stud- ied and grown in cultures at the installation included typhus, anthrax, cholera, bubonic plague, tetanus, small- pox, botulism, tick encephalitis, and tuberculosis. The facility's labs had the capability of producing up to eight tons of bacteria per month. In these labs, researchers attempted to develop an "anthrax bomb" and exploded two thousand such bombs in lab experiments.

Professor Sheldon Harris displays photos of skulls of some of the victims of Japan's World War II biological warfare experiments.

But Ishii wanted to do more than just lab research. His country was at war with other Asian nations, and he knew it would be only a matter of time before Japan went to war with the United States and its allies. He wanted to perfect his biological weapons so that Japan could use them in actual warfare, which meant that these devices would have to be tested on human beings.

Beginning in the early 1940s, therefore, Japan's biological facility began tests on human subjects. The Japanese chose prisoners of war, mostly Chinese but also some Americans, British, and Australians. In one test, the prisoners were fed food containing cultures of botulism to see how long it would take them to die. In another gruesome experiment, prisoners were tied to stakes and exposed to a bomb containing gas gangrene germs. One witness later remembered that the guards covered the prisoners' bodies with metal screening except for their buttocks, which remained exposed. When the bomb exploded, metal fragments struck the exposed area and the victims were infected by and died from gas gangrene within a few days. The Japanese also injected test subjects against their will with anthrax, cholera, bubonic plague, and many other diseases. In all, more than ten thousand war prisoners died in these terrible experiments.

While these tests continued at Unit 731's biological warfare complex, technicians conducted some grisly and decidedly unethical experiments in the field. Chinese officials reported that Japanese planes flew low over Chinese villages and dropped bags of rice and wheat mixed with fleas that had been purposely infected with bubonic plague. The planes delivered an estimated 15 million plague-ridden fleas in this manner. It is not certain how many Chinese actually died during the experiment, but Chinese officials recorded more than seven hundred plague deaths.

Anthrax Island

Japan was not the only nation to develop biological weapons. During the 1930s and 1940s, Great Britain, the Soviet Union, and the United States also launched biological weapons programs. Each country, convinced that its enemies might be making such weapons, raced to develop its own capabilities.

The British feared that Germany might use biological weapons against them, and so they spent a great deal of money on their own program. Like researchers in other countries, the British continued to explore the possibilities of using anthrax. Sometimes the experiments backfired. In 1942, for example, British researchers exploded their own anthrax bomb near a herd of sheep on the Scottish island of Gruinard. Afterward, they buried the sheep by using a conventional bomb to start a landslide, but the blast blew one of the infected corpses into the sea. The dead sheep soon floated to the coast of Scotland, where many local animals contracted anthrax. Later, a Scandinavian couple

An Aborted U.S. Plan to Use Bio-Weapons

During World War II, fearing the use of biological weapons by Japan and Germany, the United States launched a large-scale effort to develop such weapons of its own. In this excerpt from their book The United States and Biological Warfare, *Stephen Endicott and Edward Hagerman describe the first time that American military leaders actually contemplated using these devices.*

[It was] in the wake of [Nazi] General Erwin Rommel's pummeling of U.S. forces at Kasserine Pass in North Africa in February 1943. The Americans became concerned that this victory might encourage Fascist Spain to join the Axis alliance. [American scientific adviser Stanley P.] Lovell, together with scientists of the Canadian bacteriological warfare program, came up with a scheme in which mixtures including grains attractive to houseflies would be molded into the shape of goat dung, infected with psittacosis and tularemia bacteria, and dropped from planes throughout the country. The resultant preoccupation with disease was intended to draw attention away from interference with the U.S. war effort. [However,] before the military command had to make a decision on [the plan] . . . Rommel was in retreat and the plan was dropped.

A British official poses by a warning on Gruinard Island, which was contaminated with anthrax spores in the 1940s.

accidentally landed on the island after misreading their sailing charts and they, as well as their dog, contracted anthrax and died.

Over the course of decades, British decontamination experts regularly explored the island, testing to see if the anthrax spores were still dangerous. By the late 1970s, these technicians concluded that about three or four acres of Gruinard's 550 acres were still contaminated. In 1986, scientists used a mixture of chemicals and seawater to kill the remaining spores. Although British officials say the island is now safe, people on the nearby Scottish coast still refer to Gruinard as "Anthrax Island."

Soviet and American Experiments

During the 1940s the Soviets and Americans also conducted biological weapons experiments, and like the Japanese, the Soviets sometimes used human subjects. In 1941 the Soviets conducted experiments on political prisoners in Mongolia. According to an intelligence expert who investigated the tests, the prisoners were chained and made to sit in a tent; beneath the floor, which was made of wire mesh, the researchers had placed rats infested with fleas carrying bubonic plague germs. The prisoners contracted the disease, soon after which some of these men escaped. They then infected some nearby Mongolian villages, where an estimated four to five thousand people soon died of bubonic plague.

Meanwhile, between 1942 and 1945 the United States invested more than $40 million in biological weapons research. A large portion of this money went toward building a weapons plant in Vigo, Indiana, which when fully operational had the capability of producing up to 1 million biological bombs per month. In 1944 and 1945, German and Japanese officials accused the United States of dropping biological crop-killing bombs on their countries, but these charges were never proven. At the end of the war, the U.S. government sold the Vigo plant to a medicine manufacturer. But U.S. biological weapons research continued (as it did in Britain, the Soviet Union, and other countries). In a number of top-secret experiments, U.S. researchers actually tested biological agents on the unsuspecting populations of some American cities. In 1966, for instance, a biological agent called *Bacillus subtilis* was released in the New York City subway system. The test's results showed that releasing an agent in only one subway station could infect the entire underground system, thanks to the effects of the trains pushing the contaminated air through the tunnels. (The number of people infected in the experiment is unknown.)

In these same years, knowledge of germs was increasing rapidly. With the invention of even more powerful microscopes came a better understanding of viruses and their potential as lethal weapons. So biological warfare specialists began to work with such viral diseases as Rocky Mountain spotted fever, dengue fever, and Rift Valley fever. The planes, missiles, and other devices that could conceivably be used to deliver biological weapons to their targets also became more sophisticated.

By the late 1960s scientists and military experts in many countries warned that a biological war was a real possibility. They said that such a war might wipe out large segments of humanity. Consequently, government leaders around the world came under increasing pressure to eliminate this threat. In 1969 President Richard Nixon ordered all U.S. biological weapons to be destroyed, and soon afterward, on April 10, 1972, the United States, Soviet Union, and eighty-five other countries signed the Biological Warfare Convention. This agreement, which was ratified by the United Nations, banned the use of biological weapons in war.

But the agreement did not end the threat of biological weapons. Although it prohibited the use of such weapons, like the Geneva Protocol it did not ban all research. The United States insisted that the Soviet Union was continuing to study the military uses of

A group of British students protests outside of Britain's Porton Down Germ Warfare Station in 1963.

germs in violation of the Biological Warfare Convention. The Soviets denied this charge, but in fact they still had six research facilities and five weapons production plants in operation, employing a total of at least fifty-five thousand scientists and technicians. The existence of this program was revealed to the world in 1979 when a biological weapons factory in the Soviet town of Sverdlovsk accidentally released deadly anthrax spores. At least sixty-four people died and livestock located up to thirty miles from the leak were infected. According to Soviet witnesses, medical authorities burned the bodies of the dead, and bulldozers stripped away the contaminated topsoil.

After the collapse of the Soviet Union during the early 1990s, some of its biological weapons facilities were shut down; others remain operational but now only store old supplies of germ cultures rather than make new ones. However, officials in many countries are worried that some of the scientists who once worked in the Soviet germ-warfare program might be helping nations such as Iraq, Iran, and North Korea to build their own secret biological weapons programs. Of particular concern is Iraq, ruled by absolute dictator Saddam Hussein. In 2002 the United States called attention to Saddam's production of weapons of mass destruction, saying that he might use them on his neighbors or perhaps against U.S. interests or allies. Weapons inspectors authorized by the United Nations entered Iraq in November 2002 looking for such weapons. The United States and its allies warned that if Saddam hindered the inspectors or hid bio-weapons from them, these nations might attack Iraq and force Saddam from power.

The Threat of Bio-Terrorism

In addition to the threat of biological weapons from individual nations, there is also a growing threat from terrorists, either working alone or in groups, who might use such weapons. Some such groups have already attempted to manufacture their own biological devices. In 1974, for example, forty-eight Italians were arrested on charges that they had purposely placed cholera cultures in Italian public water sources the year before. And in 1980, French police found evidence that the Red Army Faction, a German terrorist organization, was working on biological devices. The terrorists were making botulinum toxin, a poison given off by bacteria, in a bathtub in a French apartment.

The first known full-blown bio-terrorist attack occurred in 1984 in Wasco County, east of Portland, Oregon. A local cult known as the Rashneeshees, which had an ongoing dispute with county officials, contaminated salad bars in ten restaurants with salmonella, a germ that causes severe food poisoning. In all, 751 cases of the sickness were reported. Luckily, there were no fatalities.

Bio-Terrorists Strike in Oregon

In this excerpt from Germs: Biological Weapons and America's Secret War, New York Times *correspondent Judith Miller and her colleagues recall the beginning of the 1984 outbreak of salmonella poisoning in Oregon that later proved to be the result of a biological attack by a local cult.*

On September 17, the Wasco-Sherman Public Health Department received a call from someone who complained of gastroenteritis [severe stomach upset] after eating at [a local] restaurant. . . . In the next few days, the department received at least twenty more complaints, involving two more restaurants. Less than forty-eight hours after the outbreak began, a pathologist at Mid-Columbia Medical Center had determined from a patient's stool that the bacteria making

people sick was salmonella, one of nature's hardiest germs, though infection usually is not fatal. . . . On September 21 . . . [there was] a second wave of reports involving people who had fallen ill at ten different restaurants. . . . For the first time ever, all of Mid-Columbia's 125 beds were filled; some patients had to be kept in corridors. Many were angry and hostile, and very frightened. . . . Violent patients and their families demanded their test results; some even threw stool and urine samples at the hospital's doctors. . . . By the end of the outbreak, almost a thousand people had reported symptoms . . . [and] 751 were confirmed to have salmonella.

Perhaps partially inspired by the Rashneeshee attack, in March 1990 a Japanese cult known as Aum Shinrikyo grew some botulinum bacteria in a lab hoping to use it to terrorize people. However, the group was unable to turn its cultures into an effective weapon. When, in April, it sprayed the germs into the air in downtown Tokyo and at U.S. naval bases in Japan, the microbes were not concentrated or potent enough and therefore caused no fatalities. Aum Shinrikyo also tried culturing anthrax and stealing Ebola viruses from an African lab, but both of these ventures ended in failure.

More successful was the anthrax attack that created death, havoc, and fear in the United States late in 2001. Letters containing deadly anthrax spores were delivered to the *New York Post*, NBC anchorman Tom Brokaw, and U.S. senators Tom Daschle and Patrick Leahy. None of these people were infected, but twenty-three people

Police seize hundreds of drums of dangerous chemicals from one of the facilities used by the Japanese terror cult Aum Shinrikyo.

contracted anthrax, five of whom died from the disease. Most of the victims apparently came into contact with the spores through cross-contamination, when some of the tiny particles leaked from the four envelopes between the times they were mailed and the times they reached their destinations. The terrorist (or terrorists) responsible for the attack has not yet been caught.

Such attacks, as well as the biological weapons threat posed by counties such as Iraq and North Korea, worry government officials and ordinary citizens alike around the world. The capability to make and deliver such devices seems to be growing and spreading. Responsible, humane nations and peoples want to ensure that these terrible germ weapons are never used again, especially on a large scale. However, with terrorist groups flourishing more than ever before, this effort is bound to be daunting and will certainly constitute one of the biggest challenges faced by human civilization during the twenty-first century.

Developing Constructive Uses for Germs

During the twentieth century, scientists discovered many innovative ways to use germs to make people's lives better. Germs are now regularly used to treat sewage and to control insects, and they are also used in the mining of uranium and copper. In addition, researchers are experimenting with using germs to clean up disastrous oil spills. In other experiments, germs are being tested on plants and crops to make them more resistant to disease. Scientists are constantly working to improve and expand these and other germ-based technologies.

Treating Sewage with Microbes

Sewage treatment is one of the largest and most widely used of these germ-based technologies. Sewage is the mixture of water and solid waste materials that people routinely discard each day, including all of the substances that go down toilets as well as through bathtub, sink, and street drains. The solid parts of sewage make up less than one-tenth of 1 percent of the total; the rest is water. Yet in a large city, as many as one thousand tons of these solid materials, called sludge, can build up in a single day. Scientists and engineers regularly treat, or purify, these wastes before disposing of them.

Germs can be useful in this disposal. This is because certain microbes in the environment feed on and digest sludge, turning much of it into harmless substances such as water, carbon dioxide, and various alcohols. Nearly all major cities in the United States now have sewage treatment facilities where germs have been added on a large scale to purify wastes. (Unfortunately, this is not the case in most other countries. For instance, more than 80 percent of the 125 largest cities located along the coasts of the Mediterranean Sea release untreated sewage directly into the sea.)

Germs in Sewage Treatment

New uses for germs are being found every day. One of the most promising is the use of germs to treat sewage, turning much of it into harmless substances such as water and carbon dioxide.

Since different types of germs are used in this process, it is necessary to separate the solid waste, or sludge, from the liquid waste. The two types of waste are then treated differently.

(A) Sludge: Raw sewage is pumped into a sedimentation tank, where the sludge settles to the bottom of the tank. Here, special germs begin to digest it (1). The sludge is then pumped into a special digestion tank, where still other germs continue to break it down (2). The digested sludge is no longer toxic and is removed for disposal (3). Some of it is dried, sterilized, and then used as fertilizer for gardens and farms.

(B) Liquid waste: Liquid waste is separated from solid waste (1A). The liquid is exposed to air (2A). This process, called aeration, speeds the growth of specific kinds of germs. These germs digest small solid waste products floating in the water. The digested solid waste is removed for disposal (3A). The remaining liquid is pure enough to release into an ocean or river without polluting it (4A).

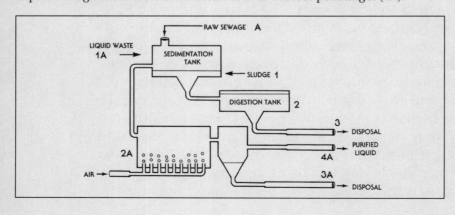

The first step in modern sewage treatment, called primary treatment, separates the sludge from the liquid components of the sewage. The raw sewage is pumped into large open tanks, where the solid materials slowly settle to the bottom. During this process, germs begin to digest some of the sludge. The next phase, called secondary treatment, is usually accomplished in two steps. In the first, the liquid portion of the sewage is aerated, or exposed to large amounts of air. The oxygen in the air encourages specific germs to grow quickly and digest particles of waste floating in the water. In the second step of secondary treatment, the solid wastes are pumped into special tanks. There, other kinds of germs digest and break down the sludge. One by-product created by this digestion is methane, a burnable gas. Many sewage treatment plants capture the methane as it is released and use it as a fuel to help run their machinery.

Scientists are constantly working to produce new strains of bacteria and other germs that will digest sewage more efficiently. One new process is called tertiary treatment. It combines germs and chemicals to purify liquid wastes so thoroughly that they can be recycled as drinking water. Presently, this is a costly process, but wastewater treated in this manner is already being used to irrigate crops in many areas of the United States.

New Ways to Eliminate Insect Pests

Another constructive use for germs is the elimination of insect pests. During the twentieth century, most insecticides—substances that kill insects—were chemical sprays. Chemical agents such as DDT effectively kill insects, but these chemicals often remain in the soil as toxic pollutants, and the poisons eventually enter streams and contaminate fish and other food sources used by animals and people.

As an alternative, germs can be used to kill insect pests without causing environmental pollution. The

Workers administer germ-based insecticides to crops. The pests ingest poisonous substances produced by bacteria and die before damaging plants.

German scientist G. S. Berliner first proposed the idea during the early 1900s. He noticed that certain kinds of bacteria destroyed moth caterpillars, which destroy crops; but the way the bacteria did this was not well understood at the time, and the idea was largely forgotten until the 1970s and 1980s. Scientists eventually learned that the bacteria Berliner observed produce highly poisonous substances during the reproduction. These poisons accumulate on plant leaves and are ingested by the caterpillars of moths, butterflies, and related insects. Once inside the digestive tract, or gut, of the caterpillar, the poisons dissolve the gut walls; and the insect soon becomes paralyzed and dies.

To make the germ-based insecticides, scientists grow large cultures of bacteria and harvest them at the time when they are producing the poisons. The bacteria are dried and made into a powder that can be dusted onto crops by ground-based machines or airplanes. Pests such as tomato hornworms, gypsy moth caterpillars, alfalfa caterpillars, and cabbage worms are regularly controlled using this method.

An important advantage of microbe-based insecticides is that they appear not to affect plants and other animals. In addition, the poisons break down quickly into harmless substances and do not accumulate in the soil, which makes this method environmentally safe. In fact, farmers have reported such a high rate of success with this approach that scientists are experimenting with bacteria that might be used to kill other kinds of insect pests.

Oil-Eating Germs

Just as promising as germs that kill insects are germs that eat oil. Scientists have long known that certain kinds of germs consume petroleum and break it down into simpler, harmless substances, a process known as biodegradation. This process occurs constantly in nature but happens randomly and very slowly, so it does not have much immediate impact on large oil spills.

It was not until the 1980s that researchers seriously considered creating concentrated batches of germs to fight oil spills. There were several reasons why this technique was not tried sooner. For one thing, scientists were not sure how these germs could be delivered effectively into a spill. Just sprinkling them onto an oil slick would not work because the action of waves and currents

Germs that Eat Oil

Scientists have long known that certain kinds of microbes consume petroleum, helping biodegradation, the natural process in which complex substances, including those made by humans, break down into simpler ones. So it seemed like a good idea to put germs to work fighting oil spills. In 1989 researchers took advantage of the notorious oil spill created when the tanker *Exxon Valdez* ran aground in Alaska. More than eight hundred miles of coastline were fouled with crude oil, and thousands of animals were killed.

To combat the spill, researchers placed sacks of biodegradable fertilizer containing microbes on the bottoms of inlets, as well as on the beaches, along the affected coast. The idea was to allow the actions of waves and tides to flush through the fertilizer and spread the germs around the area. Over time, the germs multiplied and began breaking down the petroleum into less toxic substances. The experiment was eventually pronounced a success, and microbes have since been used in a number of other oil cleanups.

quickly disperse the germs. There was also the problem of having the germs ready at the right time and in the right place, since oil spills are usually accidental and their location cannot be predicted.

The first major use of germs to fight a big oil spill occurred in 1989 when the oil tanker *Exxon Valdez* hit a reef in Prince William Sound in Alaska, spilling millions of gallons of crude petroleum. Researchers grew large masses of oil-consuming bacteria in sacks of fertilizer, which, when placed in the oil-fouled water, safely eliminated a large portion of the spill. The only major drawback of this method is that it works very slowly. Two to five years are needed to significantly reduce the amount of oil in a large spill. So scientists are currently attempting to grow new strains of bacteria that eat oil faster.

Emerging Germ-Based Technologies

Each year, modern science finds new ways to use germs productively. Some of these uses, like cleaning up oil spills, are human refinements of already existing natural processes. Another such example is the use of germs in mining technology. During the thousands of years that copper has been mined, miners were unaware that the mining process was aided by germs. Scientists discovered this phenomenon in 1957. At that time, they learned that the mining process would be impossible without the actions of certain rock-eating bacteria. The bacteria, called *Thiobacillus ferrooxidans*, consume the rust that forms in deposits of iron and sulfur. Armed with this knowledge, mining engineers have significantly improved copper-mining technology.

The engineers grind up rocks containing copper and other minerals and throw them into a pit called a dump. The *Thiobacillus* bacteria already exist in these rocks and multiply in the dump. The engineers then pour a mixture of water and a powerful acid into the

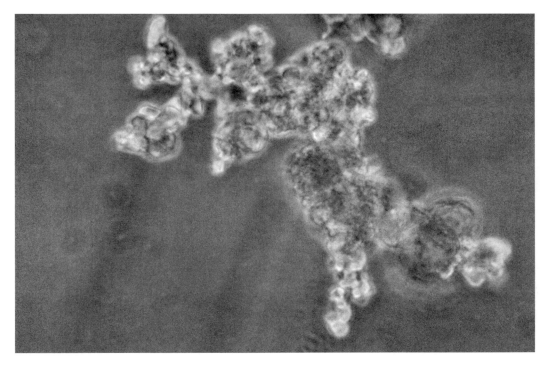

dump. As the acid circulates through the copper-bearing rocks in the dump, the bacteria cause certain chemical reactions to take place, one of which separates the copper from the iron, sulfur, and other minerals in the rocks. Separating the copper from the rock allows it to be more easily collected. Engineers have learned to use similar processes utilizing different bacteria for extracting manganese, uranium, and other metals from rocks.

This bacterium, magnified 500 times, is an example of the rock-eating variety known as Thiobacillus ferrooxidans.

While germs offer great promise in the environment, scientists have also made efforts toward finding new ways of using germs to benefit daily human life. The world's population is rising steadily, and new sources of protein are increasingly in demand. Using germs to produce protein may be one way of meeting that demand. Protein makes up about 50 percent of the body tissues of animals and people and is an essential part of any diet, as meats, dairy products, vegetables, and fruits all contain various types of proteins.

Scientists have learned to mix certain germs with carbon-rich materials such as alcohol, petroleum, and wood pulp in order to produce crude proteins. As the germs consume these materials, chemical reactions take place that produce such proteins. Germs reproduce very quickly, which means that a culture can double in weight in a few hours and sometimes in an hour or less. Therefore, this method can make large

Earth Germs in Space?

With all the modern ways that humans are learning to manipulate microbes, care must be taken to make sure they do not spread to places where people do not want them. This is especially true in the case of spacecraft landing on and possibly contaminating other worlds, as discussed here by John Postgate in his thoughtful book Microbes and Man.

If man goes into space, microbes go too. You cannot produce a germ-free human; moreover, even if you could, he or she would probably die of obscure kinds of malnutrition. Anything people handle, indeed anything that emerges from the biosphere, is contaminated by microbes. For this reason both Russian and American space agencies have been at pains to sterilize equipment sent up outside the planet's atmosphere. But a space probe in fact crashed accidentally on Venus and the question of how efficiently it was sterilized was a matter of considerable concern until [scientists learned that Venus's surface is hot enough to kill the germs]. But it would be a tragedy if the moon and Mars became contaminated by terrestrial [Earth-borne] microbes before a proper evaluation of indigenous [native] biological conditions there could be made. For terrestrial microbes might swamp, and conceivably eliminate, indigenous populations [of germs and other life-forms]. . . . Then one could never be sure that the microbes one found had not arrived with the early moon or Mars probes [or that they had evolved there on their own].

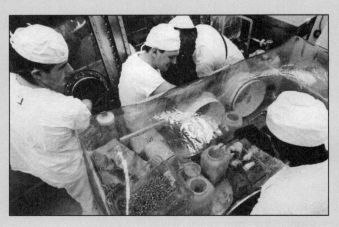

Technicians at the Houston Space Center prepare germ-free mice for contact with astronauts.

quantities of protein in a short amount of time. Proteins produced in this way are not yet widely used by humans, but many animal feeds are currently made by mixing germs and alcohol.

Other modern uses for germs are the result of innovative technologies created by human beings. For instance, scientists have invented new ways to make many medicines and drugs from germ cultures. Also, germs are routinely used to produce steroids, which promote muscle growth, and birth-control pills. One of the newest germ technologies involves genetic engineering, which is the manipulation of genes, the tiny elements within cells that carry the blueprints of life. Scientists are finding ways to change these genetic blueprints in germs, the goal being to create totally new strains of germs that will have certain improved characteristics. For instance, a manufactured germ strain might be able to eat more oil than a naturally existing strain.

Such genetically manufactured germs are already being used in a wide range of products. One new germ makes plants and crops more resistant to disease, while others are used in the production of artificial skin to heal burns and other wounds. Genetic engineering of germs is also used in recreational products. One new germ, for example, produces a protein that makes water freeze at higher-than-normal temperatures. This is currently being used to create artificial snow at ski resorts in the United States and Europe.

There is no doubt that as new and better lab instruments and techniques are discovered, knowledge about germs will increase. People will continue to find novel ways to use germs to improve the quality of human life. Eventually, it may even be possible to completely eliminate or control the germs that cause disease. But there is still much to learn. The oldest and simplest of nature's creatures have not yet given up all their secrets to the people who peer intently at them through the lenses of microscopes.

Notes

Introduction—An Invisible World Revealed

1. Arno Karlen, *Man and Microbes: Disease and Plagues in History and Modern Times*. New York: Putnam, 1995, pp. 14, 18–19.
2. Karlen, *Man and Microbes*, pp. 20–21, 23.
3. Karlen, *Man and Microbes*, p. 38.

Chapter 1—Early Attempts to Explain Disease

4. Thucydides, *The Peloponnesian War*, trans. Rex Warner. New York: Penguin Books, 1972, p. 152.
5. Quoted in Rosemary Horrox, ed., *The Black Death*. Manchester, England: Manchester University Press, 1994, p. 17.
6. Quoted in David Herlihy, *The Black Death and the Transformation of the West*, ed. Samuel K. Cohn Jr. Cambridge, MA: Harvard University Press, 1997, p. 24.
7. Quoted in Horrox, *The Black Death*, pp. 55–56.
8. Herlihy, *The Black Death and the Transformation of the West*, p. 25.
9. Boccaccio, *The Decameron*, trans. Mark Musa and Peter Bondanella. New York: W. W. Norton, 1982, p. 9.
10. Philip Ziegler, *The Black Death*. New York: Harper and Row, 1969, p. 279.

Chapter 2—The Modern Discovery of Germs

11. Barry E. Zimmerman and David J. Zimmerman, *Killer Germs: Microbes and Diseases That Threaten Humanity*. New York: McGraw-Hill, 2002, p. 10.
12. Quoted in Theodor Rosebury, *Life on Man*. New York: Viking, 1969, p. 14.
13. Quoted in Rosebury, *Life on Man*, p. 9.

Chapter 3—The Germ Theory Proven at Last

14. Quoted in Gwendolyn R.W. Burton and Paul G. Engelkirk, *Microbiology for the Health Sciences*. Philadelphia: Lippincott, Williams, and Wilkins, 2000, p. 15.
15. Zimmerman and Zimmerman, *Killer Germs*, p. 118.

Chapter 4—Disease Detectives Track Down Germs

16. Quoted in Kaari Ward, ed., *Great Disasters: Dramatic True Stories of Nature's Awesome Powers*. Pleasantville, NY: Reader's Digest, 1989, p. 190.
17. Quoted in Peter Jaret, "The Disease Detectives," *National Geographic*, January 1991, p. 32.
18. Quoted in Jaret, "The Disease Detectives," p. 34.
19. Quoted in Ward, *Great Disasters*, p. 115.

Chapter 5—A Host of Beneficial Germs

20. Quoted in Rosebury, *Life on Man*, p. 43.

Chapter 6—Germs as Weapons: Biological Warfare

21. Quoted in Robert Harris and Jeremy Paxman, *A Higher Form of Killing: The Secret Story of Chemical and Biological Warfare*. New York: Hill and Wang, 1982, p. 70.
22. Jeanne Guillemin, *Anthrax: An Investigation of a Deadly Outbreak*. Berkeley and Los Angeles: University of California Press, 1999, p. 6.

Glossary

algae: A class of plantlike living things that includes microscopic germs that absorb sunlight and carbon dioxide and give off oxygen.

anthrax: A deadly disease that spreads by releasing spores and usually strikes cattle and other grazing animals; it can also infect humans, and producers of biological weapons often consider it preferable to most other diseases for such weapons.

antibodies: Proteins manufactured by the body's white blood cells to defend against invading disease germs.

antiseptic: A germ-killing agent.

bacteria: Small germs that live almost everywhere in nature and reproduce by splitting in half; the specific study of bacteria is called bacteriology.

biogenesis: The scientific principle that holds that all living cells grow from other living cells.

biological weapons: Also called bio-weapons; devices designed to kill and injure people by infecting them with dangerous disease germs.

bubonic plague: Also known as the Black Death; a dangerous disease that usually infects fleas, which carry the contagion to mammals, including humans. A massive epidemic of the plague wiped out millions of people in Europe during the Middle Ages.

culture: A laboratory growth of germs for medical study or use.

curd: The lumpy consistency of sour milk and other dairy products.

epidemiology: The study of the manner in which diseases spread through a living population and/or the environment. A person who specializes in epidemiology is an epidemiologist, frequently called a disease detective.

fermentation: The process in which various microbes cause plant and animal products to undergo a change, usually a souring, as in the transformation of grape juice into wine or milk into buttermilk.

fission: A process in which a germ (or some other thing) divides in half.

fungi: A class of plantlike living things that includes both mushrooms and microscopic germs that cause dead plants and animals to decay.

germ theory: The concept that germs cause disease.

immune response: The body's defensive reaction to harmful substances that invade it from the outside.

immunity: The process by which the body resists disease.

immunology: The study of the process of immunity and the prevention of disease. A person who specializes in immunology is called an immunologist.

microbe, or microorganism: A germ. The study of microbes is called microbiology.

mitosis: The process in which the nucleus of a microbe or other single-celled organism splits in half.

parasite: A living thing that infests and lives off of another living thing.

pasteurization: A process named for French researcher Louis Pasteur in which food products such as wine and milk are heated to a temperature that kills any harmful germs they contain.

photosynthesis: The natural process in which algae and most plants take in carbon dioxide and sunlight and give off oxygen as a by-product.

protozoa: Large germs that live in water or other liquids. They have some internal structure, including a nucleus in the center.

sludge: The solid portion of the waste materials people flush down their toilets.

spontaneous generation: A theory, disproved during the 1800s, that held that living things could spring into being or grow seemingly out of nowhere.

spores: Tiny particles given off by fungi during reproduction. Each spore grows into a new fungus.

strain: A variation of a specific kind of disease germ.

vaccine: A substance that provides protection against a specific disease by triggering the body's natural immune system without passing on the disease itself.

viruses: Extremely tiny germs that invade plant, animal, and human cells and sometimes cause serious diseases.

FOR FURTHER READING

Molly Bang, *Chattanooga Sludge: Cleaning Toxic Sludge from Chattanooga Creek*. New York: Harcourt Brace, 1996. Written for basic readers, this is the story of how a scientist cleaned up a polluted waterway using simple bacteria. Highly recommended.

Melvin Berger, *Germs Make Me Sick*. New York: HarperCollins, 1995. Tells how bacteria and viruses spread infection and how the human body fights back. A very good book.

Jack Brown, *Don't Touch That Doorknob! How Germs Can Zap You and How You Can Zap Back*. New York: Warner Books, 2001. An excellent introduction to the subjects of germs and infection for young readers.

Mark. P. Friedlander, *Outbreak: Disease Detectives at Work.* Minneapolis: Lerner, 2000. A fact-filled volume explaining how scientists and doctors trace the source of disease epidemics and stop them from spreading.

Ann Fullick, *Louis Pasteur*. Crystal Lake, IL: Heinemann Library, 2000. The life of the great scientist who helped prove the germ theory of disease and also developed the first attenuated vaccines is effectively covered in this readable biography.

James Quigley, *Johnny Germ Head*. New York: Henry Holt, 1997. A cute, off-beat story of a little boy who imagines large germs are lurking all around him. The tale is fictional but contains accurate information about germs and how they can make people sick.

Tom Ridgway, *Smallpox*. Brookshire, TX: Rosen, 2001. An up-to-date synopsis of the history of one of the worst diseases in history, with a detailed section on how Edward Jenner developed the first vaccine.

Tony Ross, *Wash Your Hands*. La Jolla, CA: Kane Miller Books, 2000. A little princess learns that she must wash her hands to keep germs from making her sick. A nice introduction to disease germs for basic readers.

Robert Snedden and Steve Parker, *Yuck! A Big Book of Little Horrors*. New York: Simon & Schuster, 1996. Contains numerous large, colorful magnified pictures of germs (and other microscopic creatures, such as dust mites). Each picture has a clearly written, accurate explanation of the "little horror."

Brian R. Ward, *Epidemic*. London: Dorling Kindersley, 2000. Like other books by this publisher, this one is beautifully illustrated with color photos and diagrams. Highly recommended for young people looking for a general introduction to the world of germs and infectious diseases.

Major Works Consulted

Books

Wayne Biddle, *A Field Guide to Germs*. New York: Henry Holt, 1995. An extremely thorough and well-written overview of the various kinds of germs and how they interact with human civilization.

Thomas D. Brock, *Robert Koch: A Life in Medicine and Bacteriology*. Washington, DC: ASM, 2000. A fine telling of the life and contributions of Koch, one of the major early proponents of the germ theory of disease and the discoverer of the microbe that causes tuberculosis.

Gwendolyn R.W. Burton and Paul G. Engelkirk, *Microbiology for the Health Sciences*. Philadelphia: Lippincott, Williams, and Wilkins, 2000. Covers nearly all major aspects of microbes, including their structure, growth, spread, causal relationship with disease, and uses in agriculture, and genetics.

Leonard A. Cole, *The Eleventh Plague: The Politics of Biological and Chemical Warfare*. New York: W. H. Freeman, 1997. An instructive and interesting study of the way various nations have recently been dealing with the emerging threat of biological warfare.

Robert S. Gottfried, *The Black Death: Natural and Human Disaster in Medieval Europe*. New York: Macmillan, 1983. One of the better books available on the catastrophe caused by bubonic plague in medieval Europe.

Jeanne Guillemin, *Anthrax: An Investigation of a Deadly Outbreak.* Berkeley and Los Angeles: University of California Press, 1999. A highly detailed account of the deadly outbreak of anthrax that struck the Soviet Union in 1979. It contains much valuable information about this dangerous disease.

E.A.M. Jacob, *Louis Pasteur: Hunting Killer Germs.* New York: McGraw-Hill, 2000. A fine, up-to-date biography of one of the greatest scientists who ever lived and an important pioneer in humanity's understanding of germs and disease.

Arno Karlen, *Man and Microbes: Disease and Plagues in History and Modern Times.* New York: Putnam, 1995. This is a fact-filled, absorbing look at the history of germ contagion on Earth, especially as it relates to human society.

John J. McKelvey, *Man Against Tsetse: Struggle for Africa.* Ithaca, NY: Cornell University Press, 1973. This well-written volume covers the efforts of modern scientists and doctors to stem the tide of deadly epidemics in Africa, including the dreaded sleeping sickness.

Judith Miller et al., *Germs: Biological Weapons and America's Secret War.* New York: Simon & Schuster, 2001. A riveting account of the developing threat of biological warfare in recent decades, including the little-publicized 1984 biological attack on an Oregon town by a local cult.

Andrew Morgan et al., *The Eradication of Smallpox: Edward Jenner and the First and Only Eradication of an Infectious Disease.* San Diego: Academic, 2000. One of the better recent books about past medical figures, this one effectively covers not only scientist Edward Jenner but also how twentieth-century researchers finally made a concerted effort to wipe out smallpox and succeeded.

John Postgate, *Microbes and Man.* New York: Cambridge University Press, 2000. This well-written, easy-to-read book provides a useful overview of the many uses and niches of germs today, including food production, industry, medicine, biotechnology, and sewage treatment.

Theodor Rosebury, *Life on Man*. New York: Viking, 1969. Despite its date, this excellent book about the historical relationship between microbes and humans is hardly dated and remains highly informative and entertaining reading. It is also notable for its many lengthy primary source quotations by scientists and thinkers of the past.

Frank Ryan, *Virus X: Tracking the New Killer Plagues.* Boston: Little, Brown, 1997. A doctor explains how epidemiologists and other experts are dealing with the threat of disease epidemics within the complex framework of modern industrial society.

Barry E. Zimmerman and David J. Zimmerman, *Killer Germs: Microbes and Diseases That Threaten Humanity.* New York: McGraw-Hill, 2002. An easy-to-read synopsis of dangerous germs, what science knows about them, how they cause disease, and the symptoms and problems associated with various major diseases. Highly recommended.

ADDITIONAL WORKS CONSULTED

Books

Boccaccio, *The Decameron*. Trans. Mark Musa and Peter Bondanella. New York: W.W. Norton, 1982.

Frederick F. Cartwright and Michael D. Biddiss, *Disease and History*. New York: Dorset, 1972.

Department of Defense, *Twenty-first Century Terrorism, Germs, and Germ Weapons, Nuclear, Biological, and Chemical (NBC) Warfare—Army Medical NBC Battlebook*. Washington, DC: Progressive Management, 2001.

Jared Diamond, *Guns, Germs, and Steel: The Fates of Human Societies*. New York: Norton, 1999.

Clifford Dobell, *Antony van Leeuwenhoek and His "Little Animals."* New York: Dover, 1960.

Joseph P. Douglass Jr. and Neil C. Livingstone, *America the Vulnerable: The Threat of Chemical/Biological Warfare*. Lexington, MA: D.C. Heath, 1990.

William Dudley, ed., *Epidemics*. San Diego: Greenhaven, 1999.

Stephen Endicott and Edward Hagerman, *The United States and Biological Warfare*. Bloomington: Indiana University Press, 1998.

Harold Faber and Doris Faber, *American Heroes of the Twentieth Century*. New York: Random House, 1967.

Dennis B. Fradin, *Medicine; Yesterday, Today, and Tomorrow*. Chicago: Childrens Press, 1989.

James C. Giblin, *When Plague Strikes: The Black Death, Smallpox, AIDS*. New York: HarperCollins, 1995.

Madeleine P. Grant, *Louis Pasteur: Fighting Hero of Science*. New York: McGraw-Hill, 1959.

Charles T. Gregg, *Plague: An Ancient Disease in the Twentieth Century*. Albuquerque: University of New Mexico Press, 1985.

Howard W. Haggard, *The Doctor in History*. New York: Dorset, 1989.

Robert Harris and Jeremy Paxman, *A Higher Form of Killing: The Secret Story of Chemical and Biological Warfare*. New York: Hill and Wang, 1982.

Robin M. Henig, *A Dancing Matrix: How Science Confronts Emerging Viruses*. New York: Vintage, 1994.

David Herlihy, *The Black Death and the Transformation of the West*. Ed. Samuel K. Cohn Jr. Cambridge, MA: Harvard University Press, 1997.

Brent Hoff and Carter Smith III, *Mapping Epidemics, a Historical Atlas of Disease*. New York: Franklin Watts, 2000.

Rosemary Horrox, ed., *The Black Death*. Manchester, England: Manchester University Press, 1994.

George C. Kohn, ed., *Encyclopedia of Plague and Pestilence*. New York: Facts On File, 1995.

Joseph B. McCormick and Susan Fisher-Hoch, *Level 4: Virus Hunters of the CDC*. Atlanta, GA: Turner, 1996.

William H. McNeill, *The Human Condition: An Ecological and Historical View*. Princeton, NJ: Princeton University Press, 1980.

——, *Plagues and Peoples*. New York. Anchor, 1998.

Ralph Mitchell, *Water Pollution Microbiology*. New York: Wiley and Sons, 1972.

John T. Nickerson and Anthony J. Sinskey, *Microbiology of Foods and Food Processing*. New York: American Elsivier, 1972.

Nina G. Seavey et al., *A Paralyzing Fear: The Triumph over Polio in America*. New York: TV Books, 1998.

Paul D. Solley and Tamar Lasky, *Investigating Disease Patterns: The Science of Epidemiology*. New York: Scientific American Library, 1995.

Thucydides, *The Peloponnesian War*. Trans. Rex Warner. New York: Penguin Books, 1972.

Marianne Tully and Mary-Alice Tully, *Dread Diseases*. New York: Franklin Watts, 1978.

René Valery-Radot, *The Life of Pasteur*. Trans. R.L. Devonshire. Garden City, NY: Garden City, 1926.

Bruce A. Voyles, *The Biology of Viruses*. New York: McGraw-Hill, 1993.

Kaari Ward, ed., *Great Disasters: Dramatic True Stories of Nature's Awesome Powers*. Pleasantville, NY: Reader's Digest, 1989.

Christopher Wills, *Yellow Fever, Black Goddess: The Coevolution of People and Plagues*. Reading, MA: Addison-Wesley, 1996.

Philip Ziegler, *The Black Death*. New York: Harper and Row, 1969.

Hans Zinsser, *Rats, Lice, and History*. Boston: Little, Brown, 1935.

Periodicals

Peter Jaret, "The Disease Detectives," *National Geographic*, January 1991.

Jay Stuller, "Cleanliness Has Only Recently Become a Virtue," *Smithsonian*, February 1991.

Pamphlet

American Council on Science and Health, pamphlet, *Eating Safely: Avoiding Foodborne Illness*.

INDEX

PICTURE CREDITS

About the Author

In addition to his numerous acclaimed volumes on ancient civilizations, historian Don Nardo has published several studies of modern scientific discoveries and phenomena. Among these are *The Extinction of the Dinosaurs*, *Cloning*, *Black Holes*, *Extraterrestrial Life*, and a biography of Charles Darwin. Mr. Nardo lives with his wife, Christine, in Massachusetts.